# The New Talkamatics:
## Easy Way to Verbal Power and Persuasion

# The New Talkamatics: Easy Way to Verbal Power and Persuasion

### Cathy Handley

Parker Publishing Company, Inc.
West Nyack, New York

©1977, *by*

## PARKER PUBLISHING COMPANY, INC.

### West Nyack, N.Y.

**Library of Congress Cataloging in Publication Data**

Handley, Cathy
   The new talkamatics.

   1. Persuasion (Rhetoric) I. Title.
PN4121.H226   808.5   76-40253
ISBN 0-13-616102-2

Printed in the United States of America

To the best talker I know:
my mother,
Aline Norvell Thompson

# What This Book
# Will Do for You

*The New Talkamatics: Easy Way to Verbal Power and Persuasion* is a total system for speaking effectively. . .a *system* of talking your way upward, not merely a group of tips.

## What the Talkamatics System Is

This new Talkamatics system has two vital parts: (1) it's a system that will aid you in speaking with power and persuasion, and (b) it's fun, fascinating and fast to learn.

And to help you learn quickly, this new system includes tested, automatic ways to achieve forceful results; target-reaching methods—to *aim* your talking and earn big rewards; and the Talkamatics real-lifers—real-life problems/solutions/how-to-do-its—to aid you tremendously in developing effective speaking.

## What the Plan of the Book Is

The two-part plan of the book is:

1. *Talkamatics Chapters 1 through 6* show you how you can talk with polish in everyday business situations.

For example, in Chapter 1 you'll discover an invaluable "artichoke" formula to banish business people's block in conversing. You'll also learn to tape-ape—tape your voice and correct any bad faults.

Chapter 2 introduces you to the 1-2-3 Magic Package module—an easy-do way to structure your remarks to talk successfully with your customers, boss and business associates.

3

A great help in speaking your way up the ladder is Chapter 3 on making, not hit-or-miss, but *winning* presentations. And in the next chapter, you'll receive do's and don'ts to help you horsetrade (negotiate) like a pro.

Have you yearned to present and sell your ideas with skill in meetings? Chapter 5 gives you some great how-to's for putting across your ideas...plus five types of common meeting birds to stay alert for.

2. *Talkamatics Chapters 7 through 12* will help you do strong speaking before small and large groups.

In Chapter 7, for instance, you'll see how to use—and invent—today's persuasive gestures, including signposting—holding up fingers to enumerate points. You'll also find a remedy to control bothersome dancing feet.

Chapters 8, 9, 10 take you step by step through a simplified way of drafting a talk, how to do failure-proof rehearsing, eight audience-pleasing tricks, and how to field a Q&A session.

Chapter 12 alone is worth the price of the book. It contains a reference gold mine—52 ideas for speech subjects and over 35 sources (many free) for illustrative material and fresh stories.

*Talkamatics'* many guides, secrets, samples and case histories (some of the names of people and places have been changed but the incidents are true) enrich this book to help you rapidly master the material.

Throughout the book are sprinkled 165 Talkamatics tips, set in italics, to flag your attention and quickly alert you to positive actions to take as well as pitfalls to avoid in talking. Finally, there's a . . .

## Bonus "Busy-Person" Ten-Minute Feature

In this especially planned book, each subhead and the Talkamatics nugget following it has been developed to take no more than ten minutes of your time—perhaps at the start of your working day. Yet they will *immediately* help you to become a more persuasive speaker.

You can, of course, also take in several pages at once for even more rapid progress; and for years you'll doubtless wish to refer to this book for a brush-up when you face a speaking challenge.

I feel certain that *The New Talkamatics: Easy Way to Verbal Power and Persuasion* can remarkably help you advance in your career and in your life. So now, let's begin.

Cathy Handley

# Acknowledgments

My deep appreciation goes to:

— the many men and women in business who showed me by fascinating example how to talk my way upward;

— my former boss and sparkling talker, the late Robert J. Weston, general manager of the building products division of Boise Cascade;

— author-teachers Louise Boggess, Duane Newcomb, Omer Henry, and Margaret Clayton for their professional encouragement and tips;

— Dr. Jerry Tarver, professor of Speech Communication at the University of Richmond, Richmond, Virginia, and founder of the Effective Speech Writing Institute, for letting me bounce ideas off him.

Cathy Handley

# Table of Contents

> Decide what you'd like to accomplish . . . Find out what the other person wants . . . After listening attentively, restate your opponent's desire and see if he agrees to your wording . . . Now describe what you desire to gain—and why . . . Listen closely to your sparring partner's remarks . . . Seize upon any possible solution the other person mentions . . . Compliment your opponent, whenever he thinks of a good idea . . . Begin to consider what-ifs . . . Continue to consider creative alternatives . . . Watch your across-the-tabler for body language that tells you what he may think but not say . . . What to concede . . . Use the criss-crossing method

> Early-bird timing . . . Test ideas . .  Innovative ideas

# The New Talkamatics:
# Easy Way to Verbal Power and Persuasion

**One**

# How Talkamatics
# Builds Your Persuasive Powers

Suppose you picked up a newspaper and read an advertisement like this:

> CAREER PEOPLE: Would you like to solve career problems by learning to talk well? Give better presentations? Make compelling speeches? Go up the ladder via speaking with professional polish?

Undoubtedly these professional benefits would appeal to you. Most of us today realize that speaking well helps escalate a career. Chauncey Depew, the great English speech authority, put it aptly: "There is no other accomplishment that any man can have that will so quickly make for him a career and secure recognition."

## Every Day You Face Career-Building Opportunities

In your daily business life you constantly face speaking opportunities for career-advancement—conferring with a co-worker, discussing a plan with your boss, "selling" a customer with a good presentation, delivering a talk which can spotlight you as unusually able in your organization, industry, club or community work.

Certainly you *meet* these career-building opportunities, but how do you *handle* them? That's what this book is all about. It employs a new fast-results, less-work talk system that makes your ladder-climbing simpler and more fun.

## Talkamatics' Fast-Results, Less-Work System

Do you recall how you can take a few basic pieces of modular furniture, recombine, restack, mix, add to them, and develop functional variety for every room in the house?

In the Talkamatics system you don't start from scratch every time you must give a presentation or talk. Instead, you master a few basic talk modules. Then by expanding, combining and adding some fresh touches, you can talk appropriately on many different occasions.

And remember—*Talkamatics tip #1: Since you use only a handful of talk modules, you save many hours of time, and much energy. You don't have to study numerous different talking techniques!* What's more, you can combine, mix, and use these basic modules to speak profitably during many years of career climbing.

## Scoring with Bull's-Eye Remarks

So now, let's exorcise a speaking plague that bothers most of us and learn how to chat about ourselves in a seemingly casual way—but one which pays personal as well as business dividends.

## The Artichoke Module for Talking About Yourself

Have you ever noticed how in everyday talking situations—from saying "Hi" to a neighbor to chewing the fat around the swimming pool—some people just don't cut it in conversation?

Have you observed there's often a Nervous Ned? An Uncomfortable Ursula? A Frozen Fred? A Shy-Glancing Sally? A Loss-for-Words Louie? A Blushing Belinda? A Put-His-Foot-in-It Paul? The club's Opportunity-Missing Ozzie?

Charlie, the Church Clam, who doesn't talk in meetings? And Clarice, the light chatter, who couldn't fall flatter...in a conversation?

Do these people need a personality revamp? A visit to a psychiatrist? Or some such? No. Nine times out of ten to come across as an agile, alert, arresting talker all these talk cripples need do is adopt Talkamatics' easy artichoke method of talking about yourself.

To show you how to do this, let's play a little scenario. We'll imagine you've just been transferred from Grand Rapids, Michigan, to Charleston, South Carolina, and you've moved into an apartment development until you find a home. You're busy but still you'd like to make some friends. How?

*Scene 1.* The first morning when you go out to your parked car, you meet your neighbor. He stows his garment bag in his trunk and you toss your briefcase in your car. Do you merely say, "Nice day. Hope it doesn't get too hot"? No. Because if you do, two months from now you'll only advance to, "Hot day. Hope it won't be a scorcher."

Instead you use the Talkamatics artichoke method to get acquainted. Remember how you eat an artichoke? You pull off a leaf, dip it in butter sauce and then enjoy it. You pull off another leaf and repeat the process. So to use this process in breaking the conversational ice you say:

"I'm Hugh Jefferson. Just been transferred here from Grand Rapids, Michigan. Work for the Southeastern Magazine Distributors, on Barkley Road. We're one of the largest magazine distributors in the country— you know, we distribute *Good Housekeeping, Field and Stream, TV Guide.* Boy, is magazine distribution growing! Each year for the past five years our business has increased 30%...."

**Talkamatics tip #2:** *The artichoke module for starting a conversation—giving concrete facts about yourself—can color a hesitant talker hep.*

Now, let's blow the whistle, pause and analyze the above talk opener. Notice, it's a series of short, concise statements, packed with information and concrete facts. But the facts are handled like grace notes in music, lightly touched upon, not explained in detail. The above opener isn't a boring digressive monologue like:

"Hi, I'm Hugh Jefferson. Hey, I sure need to wipe off my car. Couldn't find my sweater this morning. What'd you say your name was?"[Not listening.] "Well, Jack—oh, did you say it was John? Okay, could you tell me how to get to Barkley Road?"

The first version gives the listener something to comment about. As you say, "I'm Hugh Jefferson, just been transferred from Grand Rapids, work for the Southeastern Magazine Distributors...," at any point your neighbor can break in and comment about one of the *facts*. "How about that? I went to Michigan State," or "Do you know Ted Harris at Southeastern?"

Or perhaps your neighbor listens, and merely tells you his name and business. But the next time you meet he'll have some specifics to tell you about himself, or ask you about your work. During the second talk, you seed in more facts about yours truly, and he seeds in facts about himself, and before long you'll discover you've a *mucho* nice friend.

Now let's leave your about-to-be new friend and shift to another scene.

*Scene 2.* When you arrive at your new office, you find they forgot to roll out the red carpet and your boss hasn't arrived yet. So the receptionist leads you back to your new quarters. Now, you don't get an attack of shy-itis, clearing your throat and stammering, "It's a nice day," all the while waiting for *her* to ask *you* questions and draw you out. You just quickly tear off some artichoke leaves and feed 'em to her. Like so:

"Yes, my family and I really like Charleston. We're old house nuts. Like to get old houses and fix them up. When I worked in San Francisco, we bought a Victorian monstrosity and remodeled. In Chicago, we found a little 1930's bungalow and fixed it up great. Converted a mill in Grand Rapids. We're looking around here for something we can use some elbow grease on...."

Notice, you take the initiative, with your trusty artichoke leaves. Pulling 'em off and giving her some tasty nibbles.

To this frank, open manner of yours, she responds by feeding you some artichoke leaves about herself and the office. You're into an easy conversation and she'll report to the others in the office, "The new man is really interesting. Likes to fix up old houses. I think we'll like him."

*Scene 3.* Three days later you and the family attend a Thursday night spaghetti supper at the development's clubhouse. Instead of serving yourself spaghetti, then sitting like the "new people on the block" and throwing out the rather colorless remark that you've just moved here from Grand Rapids, period, you firmly turn to the person on your right and say:

"I'm Hugh Jefferson, just moved here from Grand Rapids. I'm a district manager with the Southeastern Distribution Company. We distribute all those magazines you see in the supermarket—*Good Housekeeping, Field and Stream, TV Guide.* You'd be surprised at how many magazines are sold by the average supermarket...."

By then the homemaker-Girl Scout Leader-Sunday School teacher-part-time office worker sitting next to you will say something along these lines: "How many magazines?" or "I love *Better Homes and Gardens.* Do you handle that?" or "My cousin, Gil Sanchez, works for Southeastern Distribution in the accounting department. Have you met him?"

And you're off and running in a good conversation. But the minute conversation lags you pull off another artichoke leaf...perhaps starting off on your old houses interest. As you mill around at the party and meet people, you deftly get into a conversation, using the artichoke module  And the people you talk to will respond in that way. You'll not only find people think you're interesting but you'll unearth fascinating tidbits about them as well.

*Talkamatics tip #3: When a social conversation starts to die, revive it by breaking off another artichoke leaf—more concrete facts about another of your activities.*

By handing out some artichoke leaves of *facts* about yourself, you give your listener something to tie to and keep the conversation ping-ponging along.

While many talk theorists recommend breaking the ice with remarks about the weather, the headlines, or asking the other person questions about himself, the Talkamatics system finds it's best to plunge right in with the artichoke module.

After all, you know yourself better than any other subject so you don't have to grope for words. In fast-changing situations it's hard to work in information about the country's political situation or a famine in India.

Also, if you strike out firmly and talk on your own momentum for a few statements, the person you're talking to won't feel he's being grilled. Nor will he find you a chattering egomaniac, because your recital of facts will soon have *him* asking questions, making comments, and then the conversation will progress into an absorbing exchange.

However, a few cautions about this Talkamatics artichoke module. Stick to facts. Pick out the more interesting facts. Keep them affirmative.

In other words, if you mention weather cut-ups or a business or political misfortune, don't dwell on the negative aspects but make your comments positive—what constructive things can be done.

*Talkamatic tip #4: Don't dredge up facts that depress listeners, such as you have a brimming briefcase of work or need to fix the house's plumbing.*

What about those occasions—a family reunion, a neighbor's get-together—where you don't face the problem of talking to strangers, but you find yourself facing someone pretty difficult to talk to? Will the artichoke module work? It sure will. Just start feeding him leaves of facts about some of your activities, and before you know it you're into a great two-way exchange.

What about the business area? Will the artichoke talk module also help advance your career? *You bet it will.*

## The Artichoke Way to Talk in Business

The Talkamatics artichoke module will work for you in business, as the following scenes illustrate:

*Scene 1.* You meet your boss at the elevator and your can make a lackluster impression by talking about the weather or complaining that the service shop didn't have your car ready. Or you can peel off some tasty artichoke leaves, dip them in butter and hand them to your boss for something delicious to enjoy.

So what artichoke facts will you use? Why not some industry news? Perhaps you've read in your industry's publication that a competitor, the Trans-America Distribution Company, has decided to distribute a new magazine. You bring up the subject. Your boss indicates he knew it was in the wind but doesn't know any details.

"Well, the name of the magazine will be *Lucrative Leisure*," you say. Your boss nods with interest. So you tender another artichoke fact. "News stand price, single copy, will be $3.00." Your boss whistles at the price, asks a few questions, you answer with facts, and your boss snacks and snacks and thinks you're a knowledgeable talker.

Besides a competitor's action, you can mention a personnel change, a new office building, a grand opening and so forth which you've read about in your industry newspaper. Or if you've just returned from a field trip, feed him a few business facts garnered in your trip. You can do the same thing when you talk with co-workers. The word will get around that you're worth talking to.

*Talkamatics tip #5: Your industry publication blooms with interesting facts. Harvest some to sparkle your conversation.*

*Scene 2.* A visiting fireman comes to your branch office and is scheduled to talk with you for half an hour to learn what your department's doing.

Again, pull out your Talkamatics artichoke trick and pull off a few artichoke facts about what your department does. Not too many to swamp him—just the highlights that (a) picture a worthwhile activity and (b) give the more interesting, memorable facts about your department. For example, if your department has worked out a unique, arresting way to stack magazines in supermarkets, show him this on your office mock display. If your secretary is the only person in the office who's been able to grow ceiling-high plants, show him how the plants now soundproof the noisy typing area.

After you've fed him a few artichoke delicacies, he'll feel he's learned quite a bit—and remember you distinctly and pleasurably when he returns to the home office. In fact, from such impressions often come recommendations for promotions.

**Talkamatics tip #6:** *Talking with visiting firemen—using the artichoke module—can help your career.*

*Scene 3.* Your woman boss invites you to a get-better-acquainted lunch. Most of your previous conversations have been strictly business oriented. Now, as you drive to the Holiday Inn dining room, solve the conversational problem with some Talkamatics artichoke delicacies. You know she's a swimming, opera and flying enthusiast. You could make a remark about these activities, such as, "I hear there's some great swimming these days at Myrtle Beach," or, "I understand diva Beverly Sills is coming to town next month." But this seems a little patent in talking about *her* interests, since when she invites you for a get-better-acquainted lunch, she wants a chance to size *you* up, in more relaxed surroundings. Just what kind of person are you? So put yourself on display with the artichoke leaf method. You're riding along and you say, "Hey, look at that old house. You know, my family and I are old house nuts...."

Don't give too much detail. Just a few tender leaves nicely buttered with some interesting facts. Your boss will nibble, ask a few questions, tell you about an old-house nut she knows. You throw out a few more artichoke leaves...your tennis interest...your helping with the Boy Scout drive.

Again, this is better than conversational fodder about weather, politics, taxes, the school board and so forth. And think before you throw out a critical remark about the college kids practicing yoga; your boss may look at you and say, "I'm into yoga myself"; or if you complain about the possibility of a third political party, she might say, "I'd support one...."

But if you use the artichoke method, pulling off the leaves of facts about yourself and your work, your boss thinks, "This is a pretty open, friendly person. He's given me some information about himself and the office that'll come in handy for me to know, but it's obvious he has no ulterior motive for buttering me up." She'll then respond with interesting facts about the company and a few about herself.

Remember *Talkamatics tip #7: You use the artichoke leaves as conversational starters, not an all-about-you monologue. Once a conversation's underway, let it veer off to mutually interesting topics.*

## Easily Developing the Right Voice

About now in reading this book, you may have risen, strolled outside, tried a few artichoke leaves on Syd, the sphinx, your neighbor who for the past three years has done nothing but trade weather news with you.

When you feed him an artichoke snack about a hobby of yours, Syd unsphinxes and tells you he has a hobby himself, the stock market. He's onto a small company whose stock has doubled in the past four months. He gives out some other artichoke tidbits about the stock and you're now thinking of trying a flyer in this company's stock yourself, so you feel well satisfied with your first Talkamatics gambit.

*But*, as you think of the talking ahead of you, conferences with members of your company, with customers, presentations before groups, some formal speeches, you feel a few qualms.

While you see how effectively the Talkamatics system works in sparking conversations, you may have another concern.

You may think, "Let's face it. I don't have the world's best voice. I've got a heck of a country accent, or my New England tones sound pretty stiff down here in the South. Maybe my voice will hold me back."

Not at all. Today we're living in an era with the accent on being yourself. Yesterday's admired pear-shaped tones are fortunately yesterday's. More and more, in the movies, on TV, in business, people speak naturally.

**Talkamatics tip #8:** *You no longer need to use pear-shaped tones to rate as an ace speaker.*

Everyone can speak his individual way. And many times his individual way can be very pleasing—if he clears up a few minor faults.

## Tape and Ape

Here's a target-reacher for polishing your voice. Record ten minutes of a TV voice (of your own sex) that you like. Make a typed transcript, but don't erase the tape. Record your own voice reading the transcript.

Now compare the TV voice with your own. Do you notice any of the following problem areas in your voice? For example:

—Do you speak too fast?
—Do you speak too slowly?
—Should you vary your pace?
—Should you strive for a variety of pitch?
—Do you need to put color in your words? That is, when you come to a word like "exciting" do you pronounce it so it *sounds* exciting? And when you say a word like "difficult" do you emphasize it so it *sounds* difficult?

—Do you drop word endings? Say "diggin' " for "digging" and "hope" for "hoped"?

—How about your vowels? Do you talk about writing with a "pin" or a "pen"? Pronounce person so it rhymes with "worsen" or a strange creature called a "pusson"?

You can often self-correct these problems by listening to good voices and correcting your own faults. Keep retaping your voice and you'll see you're getting better and better. And, of course, if you have a special voice problem, you'll want to consult a private voice teacher, or a university or college voice coach.

*Talkamatics tip #9: Many times in a short period of study you can tame a troubled voice.*

## Four Aids for Lowering Your Voice

Perhaps generally you speak rather well, with one exception. Your voice sounds a little higher than you like. Here's a Talkamatics module to put a little deep-well power into your voice:

1. Speak more slowly and pitch your voice lower. The faster you speak, the higher your voice goes.

2. Put your hand on your diaphragm. When you speak, feel your voice pushing out from the diaphragm. You'll talk lower.

3. Speak a little more softly, yet distinctly. When you speak loudly, your voice goes higher.

4. Relax. In Chapter 10, you'll learn how appreciation and gratitude help you relax and curtail fear.*Talkamatics tip #10: Fear and anxiety can make your voice rise. Confidence can help it become lower and sound more vibrant.*

## The Reading-Aloud Trick That Pays Quick Dividends

But you say, "Sure, I'd practice all those tips for improving my voice if I went and took voice lessons on a regular basis. But I don't have time."

Of course you don't, but you can still easily practice your speaking and make Brownie points with your spouse and kids.

How? Practice this automatic—the reading-aloud trick. When you're reading the newspaper, read it aloud to yourself—or to your spouse. Reading aloud is a great togetherness trick (marriage partners draw closer together). Also it's a great trick for learning to hang onto dropped endings and starting to make a writing "pin" sound like a "pen."

Read nursery-book stories to your kids. Or if they're older, read an adventure story, a chapter an evening. Your youngsters will enjoy a story hour. And maybe ask if they can have their friends in to listen, too. Good! Let them do so. Because you'll improve your voice even faster if you read before a group.

And as you spruce up your voice, you're setting yourself up to be a really super Talkamatics presenter, conference attender and speaker before groups. *Talkamatics tip #11: These practice read-aloud sessions will help provide you with some great rewards a little later.*

## Setting Your Goals

Now that you've learned the Talkamatics artichoke method, maybe even broken off reading this chapter to record your voice and analyze it, and are ready to get hundreds (even thousands) of dollars and several rungs-up-the-ladder benefits from this book, what goals should you set? Should you put a time limit on when you want to have "X results" from the Talkamatics system?

Yes. You should form goals and set timetables. On a piece of paper write your secret long-term goals. Don't tell these goals to anyone. Perhaps you want to run for the U.S. House of Representatives by such and such a date. Perhaps you'd like to be regional manager of your company. Perhaps you'd like to be a full professor. You know good speaking is necessary to reach these goals. ***Talkamatics tip #12: Write down these long-term goals and how soon you'd like to reach them.***

Then review them the first of every month. Check and make sure that you're taking definite steps to reach them. For example, if your long-term goal is to be a member of the U.S. House of Representatives, are you taking steps to run for a lesser elective office that conceivably could lead to running for the House? (Becoming a more effective speaker each step?)

However, don't tell your long-term goals to anyone. Not even your mate. Psychologists warn that when you tell a major goal to someone, you risk his pointing out the pitfalls in attaining your aim. Also he may suggest an alternate goal—thus complicating your choices. Faced with various choices, you may even give up your goal.

Instead, remember ***Talkamatics tip #13: If you keep your long-term goal secret from others, frequently visualizing it in your mind's eye, you have a much better chance of reaching your target.***

Now list your short-term goals and how to reach them. Perhaps you'd like to start talking well in your staff meetings, make a business presentation, and accept an invitation to make a full-fledged speech.

***Talkamatics tip #14: Write down your short-term goals, ways to achieve them, and your timetable.***

For example, you might resolve in two weeks to make a good report in a staff meeting about an assignment you've been handling, and suggest to your boss you could make a helpful presentation about the new way of stacking magazines at the next sales meeting. You might plan to contact your local school and volunteer to give the students a talk on your hobby of rock-collecting.

If your goals are for club and community service work, list steps you can take to accomplish them.

***Talkamatics tip #15: Check all your short-term goals once a week to make sure you're actively pursuing them.***

Often, telling a mate about your short-term aims can facilitate your realizing them. For example, a supportive spouse will help you find the time you'll need.

Also, plan a reward for yourself for reaching both your long- and short-term goals. You might promise yourself a European trip if you make your long-term goal of regional manager and a new tennis racket if you make a successful full-fledged speech.

*Talkamatics tip #16: Thinking about your upcoming rewards helps you reach your goals. In fact, keeping pictures of them in a notebook or file folder you use daily will spur you on.*

Alan Lakein, the expert on managing time, used the goal of a vacation to guide him to finish a book he was writing. And at one point, when the writing lagged, he went down and buttoned up the details of the trip with his travel agent. He then renewed his task of finishing the book with zest.

## Guidelines for Speaking Opportunities All Around You

As you think about your goals, think of speaking opportunities you might grab. These might include:

- Use the artichoke module to start a conversation with someone at a party.
- Volunteer to report on a new book of tennis tips at your tennis club meeting.

*Talkamatics tip #17: You find speaking opportunities all around you, fun opportunities to grow and go up the ladder as you expertise your speaking via the easy Talkamatics system in this book.*

## Today Is Day One

You're at Day One. The big adventure—putting muscle into your talking—is about to start. Throughout this book you'll find tips, modules, short-cuts, target-reachers to help you speak with punch, power and persuasion.

In the next chapter, you'll discover how to turn small talk into BIG REWARDS. So, shall we plunge in?

## Chapter Check-Back

- *Conversing socially* becomes easy with the Talkamatics artichoke module of being the first to volunteer facts about yourself—your name, business, hobbies and interests.
- *Talking with business associates* is also simple and productive when you utilize the Talkamatics artichoke system. The secret is offering concrete *facts*, not nebulous nothing remarks, about yourself or your business. Often you find these artichoke facts in your industry publication which gives information about new products, grand openings, new buildings and personnel changes.
- *Speaking affirmatively*, not negatively, is part of the new Talkamatics system. In conversation use good-news facts. Skip talk of illness, accidents, family problems. If you must comment on a disaster or business downturn, bring out the constructive side— what's being done to help things.
- *Developing the right voice* is helped by this Talkamatics taping tip: Tape a good TV voice of someone your own sex, then copy off the message and record the same message yourself. By comparing your version with the pro's, you hear in vivid sound what areas of your voice need improvement.
- *Reading aloud to your spouse* or kids is a Talkamatics trick to achieve a winner voice. As you read, work on correcting your voice warts, such as ignored word endings or off-target vowels.
- *Achieving a voice with deeper power*. It can be done. Some Talkamatics helps for lowering your voice in-

clude talking (1) more slowly, (2) more softly, (3) using your diaphragm and (4) in a relaxed manner.

- *Setting short-term goals* helps you gain speaking success. Enlist your spouse's help. Begin right now by planning timetables for your short-term goals. These might include speaking in a staff meeting, making a business presentation, and angling for an invitation to talk about your hobby to a club or school group.

- *Forming long-term goals* is important in gaining talk-power. Set your timetable and check once a month to see if you're taking definite steps toward your long-term goals. Keep your long-term goals a secret!

# Two

# Turning Small Talk into
# Big Rewards with Talkamatics

The president of a food processing company in Pennsylvania had two candidates for the position of vice president. After reviewing their backgrounds, he chose "the one who seemed stronger. Both are good thinkers. But the person I selected gets more done because he can talk well and motivate better the people who report to him," said the president.

When I was in the advertising agency business in Illinois, two young artists started with our agency about the same time. Artist Brown received promotions from bull-pen artist to associate art director to full art director and then to creative director.

Although artist Smith was considered more talented than Brown, artist Smith didn't go beyond the rank of associate art director. Why did Brown forge ahead? The agency president said, "He can get his ideas across better to clients. If Smith had Brown's ability to talk with others and explain his ideas, I'd have promoted him to the C. D. spot."

In a Nebraska business office, a glib-tongued talker was passed over for a promotion while a woman of few words was chosen. The reason? Her boss commented, "Carla doesn't say much but what she says helps increase profits."

A California pet store owner is often quoted in newspaper stories when reporters want an authoritative remark on a pet, from a terrier to an elephant nose fish.

His secret of appearing so often in the newspapers? He speaks so well in telephone interviews that the reporters, who also may check several other pet store owners, prefer to quote at length the owner who talks best.

Thus the deft talker earns far more free press publicity than owners of competitive pet stores. And this valuable publicity has helped his store grow into a chain.

All day long you're saying something. It has been estimated the average person speaks about 30,000 words every day, or about 3100 words an hour through the normal working day. How you use your 30,000 daily words—how· you say things, what you say and what you don't say—is building your success or non-success.

Is your daily talk as effective as you can make it? Talking expertly takes you up the ladder. And an essential of talking well is to sharpen your mental pencil and brief and edit your remarks.

## How to Use Pleasantly Skinny Small Talk

In the last chapter you learned how to use the artichoke module of breaking off facts about yourself, your job, your hobbies, and feeding these tasty talk leaves to people you meet in business or social situations to break the conversational ice.

However, many speaking situations are not ice breakers but ones where you wish to answer specific questions or provide information that's needed. If you handle these incorrectly, with the overstuffed remark, the weighty comment, the fat, fat, fat reply building up with dozens of words when 30 or 40 words would have done the job nicely, you contribute to today's greatly overweight talking.

And *Talkamatics tip #18: You hold yourself back in business with fatty talk.*

How do you "skinny" your small talk so it's potent and persuasive?

## The 1-2-3 Magic Package Module

In a nutshell, one secret of adroitly shrinking your small talk is to utilize the Talkamatics 1-2-3 Magic Package module. Stripped down, the module is this:

1. Your opening remark should give your statement of purpose.

2. Your second point should provide a specific—such as an example, statistic, analogy, comparison, quotation from an authority, reference to your own experience—that backs up or explains your statement of purpose.

3. Your third remark should be a restatement of your purpose and often a call for action from your listener.

Now let's look at this little wonder worker, the 1-2-3 Magic Package module, in action. Let's say you need to ask for a breakdown on an invoice your accountant has prepared. So:

1. (Your opening remark gives your statement of purpose.) "Lois, can you give me a breakdown on the Acme Engineering invoice #355? That's #355."

2. (Now you come to the second part of the Magic Package module and you make a specific statement of why you need the invoice.) "The client phoned and while he doesn't question our figures—the total amount looks fine— he'd like a detailed breakdown because he wants to share part of the cost with another department head."

3. (For the third part of the 1-2-3 Magic Package module you repeat your statement of purpose and ask for action.) "So, I'd appreciate it, Lois, if you'd break down the Acme invoice. Could I have it by noon Wednesday?"

Let's analyze. What are some of the good things about this skinny business small talk? Several, including:

1. You state clearly and briefly what you want to know.

2. In the second portion of your request, using the Magic Package module, you give a concrete reason why you need

this information. This convinces Lois so she'll act on the request. Nor will she worry, thinking she might have made a mistake in her figures.

3. Often, too, you need only give *one* specific. Perhaps you want a breakdown of the invoice for various reasons, but in this instance, one specific reason why will satisfy the accountant.

On-target speaking like the above helps you advance at a much faster clip in the business world.

## What Happens When You Wing It?

However, the majority of people don't use the handy 1-2-3 Magic Package module. Here's how an *au natural* speaker, without the Magic Package module, might handle the above request:

*Wrong:* "Hi, there, Lois. Have a big weekend? Okay, baby, pull yourself together and after you get your morning coffee—no hurry—pull out that file and dig up the invoice on the Acme Company's Lake Villa brochure. What's the invoice number? Oh, heck, I can't find the number. I just got back from out of town and my desk is a mountain of paper. But you know— that Lake Villa job.

"Boy, have I got a headache this morning—maybe I did too much gardening over the weekend. Anyway, get me the breakdown on that invoice. How soon do I need it? Oh, I don't know. Let's see. I'll be at the Gordon Company this afternoon. Then I think I'll go to that Chamber of Commerce luncheon tomorrow. Have it ready by tomorrow afternoon. Is tomorrow Tuesday? Yeah, make it Tuesday. Oh gosh, sweetheart, I don't want to press you. Make that Wednesday. What'd you say? Anthing wrong? No, the invoice looks okay. The client isn't questioning the accuracy. But you know that client, tight-fisted. He's got a chance to share the cost of the brochure with the personnel department so he wants to give the personnel manager a detailed breakdown."

Truly, this wrong version of business small-talking is far more common than the first. By comparing the two examples it's apparent that the second version, with the lack of facts, the fat of personal remarks, the repetitions, the indecisiveness, is wasteful of both employees' time.

In skinnying your small talk, constantly ask yourself, "How much do I need to say to make myself understood?" You'll be surprised how little you need to say to get your remarks across and cause people to think you're an expert talker.

## How to Beef Up Too-Sparse Remarks

Occasionally you may find you need to beef up your small talk—that you're *too* sparse a talker, that you're often at a loss for words, and this is holding you back in your career. Using the 1-2-3 Magic Package module meets this problem, too. Attending to the second part of the module, giving *specifics* about your statement of purpose, will flesh out your remarks.

**Talkamatics tip #19:** *Adding a few concrete phrases can often convey the impression that you're an especially competent talker.*

## Why a Real-Estate Saleswoman's Small Talk Brought Big Sales

When I lived on the West Coast, I heard of a Los Angeles real-estate saleswoman, we'll call her Anita Anderson, who, entering the real estate field after having been a fulltime homemaker and mother for many years, had begun to chalk up records in selling homes.

Newspaper reporters wrote feature articles about her sales volume. Other real-estate people tried to analyze her success. While Anita knew how to sell and had a pleasing personality, the thing that impressed me most was this: When a couple came to her seeking a house, after a few minutes of conversation she employed her You-Slant sentence. It was: "Is there anything really special you're looking for in a home?"

This You-Slant sentence would trigger a flash of desire from the couple. Often one or the other would say, "We'd like a fireplace," or "My husband wants to be near a golf course," or "A nice patio is what we'd like."

The reason Anita hit on this You-Slant sentence was that she thought ahead of time. She looked into her own experience and considered why people she knew *really* bought houses and came up with the conclusion that they chose one house over another similar house because it had a special feature they wanted.

Thus, in her conversation with clients she used only minimal small talk, such as where her prospects had moved from, the weather, how attractive their children were, her own domestic situation and so forth, and plunged right into the heart of what concerned her clients: her You-Slant sentence.

## When to Use the You-Slant Sentence

All around you every day you have tremendous opportunities to employ target-reachers—persuasive You-Slant sentences. Think ahead. Whom will you see today? Your boss, your co-workers, suppliers, perhaps customers. When you meet them why mention any of the random things that pass through your mind—the world situation, your delay in picking up your car at the service center, your need to take an hour or two and organize your desk.

Instead, think of the You-Slant sentences you can employ. To your boss: "I'll have that hot report for you by mid-morning" (think how glad he'll be to hear that); to a co-worker, "Here's the name of that fellow to ask for when you call the Lesly Company about servicing your machines"; to a supplier, "Everyone commented on the quick delivery you gave us on the premium order. It enabled us to distribute it at our booth at the trade show."

These are the kinds of You-Slant sentences people want to hear when you talk with them. They pack far more power than pointless comments. And these You-Slant small remarks not only will please others but will also help to bring big rewards to you in business advancement. **Talkamatics tip #20:** *Start think-editing your remarks. Use fewer words and more You-Slant sentences.* People will peg you as a strikingly accomplished talker.

## Tested Ways to Launch Specific Business Conversations Successfully

Someone once said about business remarks, "It's *starting* the conversation that's a problem." This is quite true. Weak or wrong beginnings can damage you in the business world. And most people are bothered by start-off problems in speaking.

"But," you may say, "what about the artichoke module in Chapter 1? Isn't that great for starting a conversation?" Yes, it's great for breaking the ice but you need more precise techniques in business situations where you wish to impart specific information or ask a definite question. Let's consider the following modules in launching business conversations:

**1. Start affirmatively.** In a recent study I made of 300 people, ranging from secretaries to outside salesmen who visited the office of 10 executives, 215 of the 300 callers started with a negative opening remark such as, "Sorry, I've got a cold this morning," or "Boy, what a nasty day. Ever see such bad weather?" or "I hate to tell you this but I don't have the memorandum you asked for. Could I have a day or two more?"

Checking the 85 talkers with opening affirmative remarks and the executives' reactions to them, it was found that 78 of the affirmative talkers completed their business successfully. Of the negative 215 talkers, only 63 carried out their business to a successful conclusion,

Thus **Talkamatics tip #21:** *Kicking off a business conversation on a positive note often leads to greater success.*

**2. Start without hedging or apologizing.** According to executives I've talked to, employees and outside callers will often start a conversation with "Er, ah, uh, I don't know how to say this..." or "I'm kind of at a loss for words how to begin..." or "I'm not the world's best at explaining things but...."

Obviously, if you hedge or apologize, an executive will think (a) you're trying to cover up something or (b) you don't have much speaking ability. He'll also begin to resent your taking up his time. He thinks, "Why doesn't he stay away till he can figure out what he wants to say?"

If you must tell someone something and are unsure how to phrase the remark, simply tell him. If, for example, you're an office manager and you've learned that five typewriters have been stolen and it appears one of the firm's ex-employees has taken them, without fanfare say, "Mr. Arnold, we've just discovered five typewriters have disappeared. It appears that one of our ex-employees, Bobbie Franklin, who's having financial difficulties, took them last night. We expect to recover them today." Your sympathetic but in-command-of-things voice will show compassion over Franklin's plight, yet indicate to the executive that you'll work calmly on obtaining the typewriters' return.

### 3. Start with an Other-Person Benefit.

Often you can launch a conversation with a reference to a benefit for the person you're talking to. Whenever this is possible, do so. Take the example of an engineer, Nancy Simpson, going in to brief the head of her department, Bert Elmore, on a road-building project. Two possible beginnings:

*Wrong.* "Well, Bert, maybe, despite all the delays, we'll finally make it. But wait'll you hear about this latest delay...."

*Better.* "Bert, you can turn in a good department report this month. We'll complete the Campbell Boulevard job on time...actually, it appears we'll be about four days ahead of schedule."

Nancy's first remark in the better version contains a solid Other-Person Benefit. Naturally, Bert is impressed with

Nancy's ability when she tees off with an Other-Person Benefit instead of losing her message in yak-yak.

**Talkamatics tip #22:** *Whenever you can, insert an Other-Person Benefit into your opening gambit in a conversation.*

The person you're talking to will eat it up, your dialogue will go better, and you'll rate as an excellent speaker.

## Talkamatics Tracking

A major problem in talking today is *wandering from the point.* Constantly bringing in non-related subjects causes conversational clutter and this jumbled talking fatigues your listener. Worse than that, if you practice a cluttered talk style, it mars your image and slows your upward progress in business.

But, you say, "How can I edit everything that rolls off my tongue? It's one thing to edit a letter or memo, another thing to curb a tongue."

The principle is the same. You blue-pencil with your thinking. The more you think about what you're saying— what's necessary to speak of, what isn't—the more effectively you can say it. Here are ways to think-edit and stay on the Talkamatics Track:

**Think of your subject as a railroad track** When you make remarks relating to that subject, you go straight ahead on the track.

For example, you've met with some people to talk about raising money for a town library. You've decided to discuss "How to raise money from people able to donate $1000 or more." As you talk, you're careful to think-edit, and don't even mention money-raising schemes involving people who can give smaller donations. You know that to do so brings jumble into the talk.

**Don't get derailed by someone else's bringing up irrelevant subjects.** If you've met with someone to talk about the contributors' list, he may break off and say, "By the way, any ideas on how we can publicize the new library?"

With the Talkamatics Tracking system, you answer that while you have some ideas, you'd like to talk about them at another time. "Right now, let's finish this list," you suggest.

With some people you often must put the subject back on the track—pleasantly—a number of times. But in the end, these talk track-jumpers will be happy over the progress you've made in your meeting and will boost you as a get-things-done person.

**Weed out the personal, whenever possible.** When you listen to tape playbacks of business, civic, club or meeting talks, you're struck by the time wasted on personal subjects. For instance:

Two people meet to talk about whom to tap for funds for a new library, and almost immediately their talk wanders off into personal chit-chat. Talker A says, "Sean Dorchester, the Vice President of Universal Steel, could give $1000 without any trouble." Talker B picks up and says, "Yeah, Sean plays a great game of golf, too, according to my neighbor who plays with him. By the way, my neighbor's got a terrific drive. Last week he whacked a ball...."

If Talker B had picked up on the word "trouble," and given Sean's address and telephone number, and discussed who should contact Sean, the meeting would have talk-tracked. So *Talkamatics tip #23* is *keep think-editing out time-wasting personal remarks from your talking.*

## Discarding Dum-Dum Talk

In business, club, church work, people sometimes limit themselves by employing dum-dum talk. I picked up this phrase from an executive who gave me a list of what he dubbed dum-dum talk. He included on his list of dum-dum phrases:

**Health remarks.** "Some people," noted the exec, "are always describing symptoms of sinus or headache or backache. Unfortunately, I can't do anything about their health. So why take up my time or anybody else's time with symptom chatter."

**Too much detail.** "For example, when a factory superintendent comes in to talk to me about a project he's involved in, he tells me too much. Say his subject is the installation of new machinery. He'll not only tell me about this, but he'll also tell me which employee is operating the machinery, that the employee has celebrated his birthday and plans a camping trip to Canada. I don't want to know so much detail. I need to know that the machine is installed and working properly. Period."

## Defusing an Argument the Talkamatics Way

As you go up the ladder, a serious deterrent can be a tendency to get into arguments. "You never win an argument," said one wit. So a Talkamatics automatic is never get into an argument. How?

**1. Never let yourself become emotional.** I recall being in an agency presentation in a new banking campaign with the bank's top people. They asked several questions. Curtis Farber, the bank's advertising manager, rushed to defend our agency work. Suddenly Curtis burst out with the fact that he considered the campaign highly creative and the bank officials were trying to stifle our ideas. Overcome, Curtis had to leave the room.

The agency team felt extremely unhappy about this. We were able to answer the bank officials' questions easily and gain a go-ahead on the campaign but Curtis ruined his chance of promotion. From then on, he was pegged as "emotional." If he'd merely helped answer with facts the questions about the campaign, in a few minutes he'd have received an OK.

So in a tight situation never react with emotionalism. In fact, it's good to train yourself never to show too much emotion. If you're in a hot meeting, remind yourself, "This is just the way we all feel today. Tomorrow we may feel differently about things. So why should I spin my wheels and become too emotional right now? ***Talkamatics tip #24: Always keep building up your capabilities by staying calm.***

**2. Train yourself to disagree pleasantly.** If you're talking to someone, and he presents a fact or idea with which you don't agree, go ahead and disagree. But do so amiably, in a face-saving way for him. For instance, use phrases like, "I think you have some good ideas there but I question if that marketing plan would be profitable. But it's certainly an interesting idea."

Or if someone in your department hands you a report he's written and you feel it needs more work, don't say scornfully: "This is a confusing report. I suggest you do some more work on it."

Instead, in a friendly tone, say something like: "This is a good report. It has a lot of substance but I think it needs a little more work. Why don't you go over it and put a neat summary on it?"

When the person leaves your office, he'll feel quite pleased, and in trying to put a summary on it will realize that it needs more work and he'll do it. And you've by-passed an argument.

**3. Postpone a meeting.** Often in a meeting with someone, you find the two of you are on the brink of arguing. It may be one of you has had a bad day. When someone has an out-of-sorts feeling, it's a waste of time to try to accomplish something. Unobtrusively get out of the meeting. Some excuses you can use are:

- "It's later than I thought, Joe! Can we get together tomorrow?"
- "I just discovered I left something important back in my office. Could we meet next week?"

These may seem transparent excuses as you read them but they won't seem so to the other person. You'll both have time to cool off and things will look different to both of you the next time you meet.

So you see how your Talkamatics know-how builds up. Your training in use of the module of facts in the first chapter helps you to continue to use facts in the 1-2-3 Magic Package module and others given in this chapter.

By polishing your daily small talk, you can start biting into the juicy and rewarding big business apple. But suave shooting the breeze in business is just the beginning. Making polished presentations can take you on an even more lucrative path. So for some helpful presentation pointers, read on.

## Chapter Check-Back:

- *Talking well* takes you up the ladder fast.
- *Using pleasantly skinny small talk* is often a matter of employing the 1-2-3 Magic Package module: (1) your opening a statement of purpose, (2) your second point some specific that backs up this statement, and (3) a re-statement of your purpose and often a call for action from your listener.
- *The clamming-up problem*—not enough to say—can also be handled with the 1-2-3 Magic Package module. The second part of the formula, using some specifics, antidotes much tongue-tiedness.
- *Employing the You-Slant sentence*—talking about what really concerns your listener—will help you get across your ideas with persuasiveness.
- *Launching conversations successfully* can often be done in one of these ways: starting affirmatively; starting without hedging; or starting with an Other-Person benefit.

- *Talkamatics Tracking* includes think-editing so you keep to the subject under discussion, getting other people back on the track when they talk-wander, and weeding out irrelevant personal remarks.
- *Discarding dum-dum talk* means omitting fruitless talk of health symptoms, and giving too much tiresome detail.
- *Defusing an argument* the Talkamatics way includes never becoming over-emotional. A good argument defuser is complimenting someone on some aspect of his project before you disagree with another aspect.

**Three**

# Talkamatics Enables You
# to Make Winning Presentations

Picture yourself answering the phone and it's your boss asking you to step into his office right away and present your ideas on a distribution problem.

Picture yourself receiving a promotion and your present duties increased. You must make an in-company presentation or give a presentation to a customer about a new company product.

How do you handle these presentations? Easily? Ably? Persuasively? You can if you know the Talkamatics ABC's of presenting. First, here's how to put across your ideas with the top man in your department.

## 1. Putting Yourself Over with the Boss

Every so often your boss or his secretary phones and requests you to step in for a few minutes. Usually the top guy or his amanuensis doesn't say what you'll be talking about, so remember these two Talkamatics target-reachers:

#1. Ask, "Can you tell me what the meeting will be about? That way I can bring any necessary papers."

#2. If the secretary is on the phone, often she doesn't know the meeting purpose, so rapidly make an educated guess. If, for example, you've been working on a plan for rescheduling the delivery system, gather up that pertinent file folder. Or if you're working on your department budget, take along that information. Also mentally run over the current status of other jobs you've been handling.

**Reading the mental climate.** When you enter your boss' office, quickly assess the mental climate. Does he look pressured? Relaxed? Annoyed? Unusually happy? How does he greet you? As if he wants the meeting short and to the point? Or long and thorough?

Shift into the proper gear for his mood. If he appears pressured, try to project calmness and helpfulness in your manner of speaking.

If he seems relaxed, relax slightly yourself with a pleasant remark.

*Talkamatics tip #25* is *adjust your remarks to mesh properly with your boss' mood.*

**Presenting ideas broadly.** One of the differences, employers say, between an on-his-toes employee and one not really making it is the latter's inability to make a deft verbal presentation—and a persuasive one.

One man told me, "I have a printing production manager who drops in to brief me on something in his department. And he acts like a wind-up doll. He gets talking on department details and I learn tons of things I don't need to know. Also, he often tosses something really important, like he's unearthed a great new paper source, right into the midst of a piddling recital about the department switching from a coffee to a tea break."

*Talkamatics tip #26: When your boss asks for a report on the status of a job, watch yourself. Answer his questions but answer them broadly.*

The 1-2-3 Magic Package module mentioned in Chapter 2 is an ideal method for persuasively replying to questions because (1) in your first statement you say clearly what the status of the job is, (2) you give a few specifics (which focus concretely on the subject and prevent you from sounding too airy) and then (3) you conclude by restating your first remark as, for example, the status of the job, and then add your next course of action or recommendation or ask your boss if he wishes to give you any directions.

**Employing the Magic Package module in an oral report.** Here's how you might use the 1-2-3 Magic module when you report orally:

Let's say you're the manager of a real estate housing project scheduling its grand opening. You go in to tell your boss everything's set. With the 1-2-3 Package module, you first make a statement of information or intent. For example:

1. "Just wanted to brief you on the progress of the grand opening at Myrtlewood. Everything's going great—right on schedule!"

Now, for the second part of your report, give some specifics:

2. "We're doing last-minute things. The sign department is finishing up the signs that lead to the model houses. We've hired a maid to keep things spic 'n span. The construction gang's morale is high. They're working hard, will finish on time and make their bonus."

Notice, not too many specifics. Just enough to show everything's under control. When you give too few specifics, your boss gets an uneasy feeling things may not run as smoothly as your airy report claims. If you give too much detail, he sags from all your conversational clutter and thinks you're just a "detail guy" or "too much of a technician" to go very far.

For the third part of your report, using the 1-2-3 Package module, state again that things are going well and ask if there's anything else your boss would like you to handle. For example:

3. "Yes, everything's right on schedule. And looks real good. Now is there any special directive you want to give me? Or anything else you'd like me to take care of?"

These last sentences leave an opportunity for your boss to give you steering advice or make a special request.

**When to present points in more detail.** In verbal you-to-boss presentation, sometimes he may request you to present certain points in your presentation in greater detail.

He'll cue you in on this either by asking for more details or by his obvious interest. If he suddenly becomes unusually alert and asks you to expand, then of course tell all you know about the matter.

Some occasions might be:

—You've received information that an important customer of the firm may award his account to another supplier.
—The lagging production of one department may affect production of other departments more than is current-ly showing up on the weekly progress sheets.

In situations like this, lay everything you know on the line. In fact, *Talkamatics tip #27* is *don't hold back on significant details when the boss asks for a depth-reading.*

**How to put forth an idea.** While often your presentation will cover a job in progress, sometimes you'll want to persuasively present a *new* idea.

In organizing this type of presentation module find out the facts about the situation, consider the solutions, and figure out your recommendations. For a show-you, let's say you plan to talk to your boss about the substitution of half a day off for employees in place of the annual Christmas party.

Your opening statement of the module might run:

1. "I recommend we poll the employees and find out whether they'd prefer the Christmas party or one-half day off for shopping."

The middle section of your persuasive presentation then gives specifics of why you suggest this:

2. "I'm recommending this because of loss of man hours. As you recall, last year Al Omsted got high, started to jig on a

table, fell off, and broke his leg. Because of complications he didn't return to work for seven weeks.

"The year before Carol Barkman had an accident driving home on a snowy street. She was off from work for three weeks. After our last Christmas party, six people told our nurse they became ill from eating too many goodies and couldn't come to work next day.

"Other people have told me the strain of getting their Christmas shopping done in crowded stores on weekends caused them to become so run down they had to stay home from work to recover.

"Conversations I've had with employees indicate the majority would prefer an extra half day for shopping. I believe cost-wise the half day would be more feasible than the Christmas party."

You give some figures illustrating your point and then wind up your recommendations with:

3. "So I recommend we poll the employees and find out whether they'd prefer the Christmas party or one half-day off for shopping."

Notice that the emphasis in persuasion is on what will persuade your boss. In this instance, you feel it's the loss of productive man hours. While you could have based your presentation on other reasons—such as your suspicion that many employees were simply bored with the annual party— you stress the most persuasive point to your boss: expensive absenteeism by productive workers.

During your presentation, it greatly helps to have a few visual aids to illustrate your points. (You'll find visual aids described in Chapter 5.)

For instance, in the Christmas party versus the half-day-off presentation, you might show your boss some Polaroids or a picture from the company house organ of Al with his leg in a cast and Carol in her hospital bed. Your accountant might help you work up a chart with the man hours lost because of the last Christmas party, which would contribute to an effective graphic presentation.

It's also a wise idea to leave a memo for your boss that gives even more concrete details of your point of view.

If your boss asks you questions, you can refer also to your memo for facts and figures.

*Talkamatics tip #28: It definitely will pay you to make a well-organized, persuasive presentation to your superior, whether he is the chairman of the board or the head of your department.*

I've seen a number of people go ahead by making sales presentations about various subjects. In my own case, I found when I took the trouble to present an idea to my boss, he was far more likely to buy it than if I just threw out my brainchild when I met him at the water fountain or the elevator.

One of my friends, Ward Fox, in the furniture business, received a hefty increase for presenting a new product idea to his boss.

Grayce Leveron created a job for herself when she made a well-planned, persuasive presentation to a large national association, recommending that the organization set up a centralized personnel department. Her presentation included facts and figures which showed this should be done. Her proposal was accepted and she was asked to organize and serve as the department's director.

So *Talkamatics tip #29* is *whenever possible, utilize a well-prepared presentation to give you career leverage.*

**Gaining your boss' cooperation.** When you make a report or presentation to your boss, these target-reachers will help you gain his support:

a) Find out *how* he likes you to report to him: short oral presentations, leaving with him a memo with details; a longer oral presentation, plus an explanatory memo; or a verbal presentation that covers the ground with no memo follow-up.

b) Find out *when* he likes you to make oral reports. Once a week? Twice a month? Only when something special arises?

c) When you give an oral report or presentaticn to your boss, ask if he has any input—suggestions, additions, recommendations—he'd like to make. Often your superior would like you to emphasize certain things in your follow-up activities and your query provides him an opportunity to direct you.

d) Every so often, when reporting, check to determine if you've handled an assignment to his satisfaction. Ask if he has any suggestions as to how you could improve the next job of this nature.

List your boss' interests. For example:

• Increasing company profits
• Building sales
• Keeping a lean staff
• Studying Chinese history

Whenever possible, relate a business presentation you make to increasing company profits or efficiency, building sales, and/or helping achieve a lean staff. Such tie-ins make your presentation much more persuasive. Occasionally you can make a pleasing reference to his hobbies.

## 2. Putting Yourself Across with a Graphic Presentation

Not only do you need to report to your boss, but often you need to make a presentation to a customer or to someone in connection with outside interests.

When this happens, a persuasive help is to use a target-reaching graphic display folder. This is similar to the visual presentation folder a salesman uses with customers and it can swell your presentation success by about 200%—or more.

***Talkamatics tip #30: Reinforcing what you say, with visuals, makes your presentation far better understood and remembered and thus far more persuasive.*** Also using a graphic display folder makes it easier to give a top-notch presentation. You don't forget any points or get them out of order.

Now quite possibly your company maintains an art department. If so, consult the art director about assembling a graphic folder for you.

But perhaps you may say, "My firm doesn't employ an art director. And my firm, club or civic group has a very limited promotional budget."

OK. Whether you get a professional artist's assist or do it yourself, you can assemble a graphic display folder easily and thriftily. Why? Because a graphic folder's effectiveness doesn't depend primarily on its elegant execution—though that's nice—but on what I call *smart think*. By using your smarts, figuring out what the viewer needs to know, then giving it to him, you can make a potent presentation. Here's how:

Let's say you work for a small firm that manufactures canvas accessories—including tarps; tops and windows for trucks; filtration; tents and boat covers to sell to consumer and industrial customers.

Every so often, when business slacks off, you call on some industry prospects, give a verbal sales pitch, show them a few swatches of materials, quote prices, ask for an order and depart. With this technique, your batting average ranks about 30%.

If you'd like to step up your presentation efficiency, make a graphic folder to show as you talk.

First:

**Make your shopping list.** Buy a few supplies at your stationery or office supplies stores. You should purchase:

—An 8½″ x 11″ or 11″ x 14″ presentation folder (I prefer the larger size for see-ability) with white pages covered with plastic. These folders come in two styles: notebook or easel. You'll need 10 to 12 pages. So buy the extra pages you'll need at the same time you buy the folder.

—Colored heavy paper. If you wish to use a special color scheme you may want to replace the white pages with colored ones, so purchase the appropriate colors or make them from a colored heavy paper.

—Some colored felt-tip markers. Perhaps red, blue, yellow, green and black unless, again, you wish to carry out a special color scheme. Also pick up colored tape you can use to make bar graphs, arrows, points, and 3″ x 5″ notebook.

—Ruler, Scotch tape, rubber cement, graph paper.

—Press-on alphabet letters. I prefer an assortment of sizes, including 2″, 1½″, 1″ and ½″.

**List your presentation points.** Now, jot down the major points why your customers might buy your products. Some sales points for your truck covers might include: they offer protection from theft, weather, dirt, save you money, come in a variety of colors, are custom-tailored to fit well, are guaranteed, have fast delivery, are made of specially developed wear-longer materials, leading firms use them, your company has been in business for 20 years.

**Plan your headings.** Arrange these points in the order you'll want to make them during your presentation. Knowing what to say and in what order increases your presentation's persuasiveness.

Now here's a procedure that's a Talkamatics automatic: Write short headings that indicate the point but don't explain in detail. You'll do that as you point to the heading and talk to your customer. These midget headings might include:

— Protects
— Saves money
— Colorful
— Custom-made

After you've made all your midget headings, for each one write brief reason-why subheads. In other words, the subheads will explain or substantiate your headings. For instance, under the heading "Protects," you write:

— Weather-proof
— Dirt
— Theft

Then you'll explain during your presentation that these truck covers protect loads from sun, rain, snow, dirt and theft.

You then make some brief subheads for the rest of your midget headings: "Saves money," "Colorful," "Custom-made," and so forth.

Now:

**Create your illustrations.** Consider how to illustrate each page. For "Protects" you might look through consumer and trade magazines, catalogs or advertising folders and find an open umbrella. For "Saves money" you might discover a picture of a piggy bank. Cut these pictures out. Later, you'll paste them on your presentation folder pages.

To illustrate "Colorful" you might show swatches of several truck cover materials in various colors.

Perhaps you have a midget heading that lends itself to a figure illustration. "Saves money" might be illustrated with a big "2%" you cut out of a magazine. Or you might have a subhead that lends itself to a chart, or bar graph treatment Prepare this type of illustration.

**"Thumbnail" layout.** Once you know what your heads, subheads and illustrations will be, take your pocket notebook and rough out various thumbnail layouts or arrangements of words and illustrations to a page.

*Talkamatics tip #31: For the first page of your layout put in your company's name.* In this analogy, this might be

"General Canvas Accessories." ***Talkamatics tip #32: On the second page of your layout you might want to put your company's slogan or a wrap-up statement of what your company does.*** In our analogy, this could be "Current Canvas Accessories with 1000 Uses."

Then begin to make thumbnail layouts of your main points, using headings, subheads and illustrations. Put only one main point to a right-hand page. Generally speaking, don't use a left-hand page. Material on facing pages confuses the viewer. He tends to look at one page, while you talk about the other. Occasionally you may wish to make one main point, using one heading, on two facing pages. After you've doodled a number of thumbnail layouts, choose the most attractive ones.

Use felt-tip pens or press-on letters to do your lettering. A simple lettering style is more easily read. Make your headings at least 1″ tall and your subheads at least ½″.

Another trick I've used is to place press-on letters or artwork (such as a piggy bank or umbrella I've cut out of a magazine) on the folder pages, and trace their outlines with pencil. Then I remove the letters or artwork and fill in the pencil outlines with a felt-tip pen. This gives a just-crafted look.

Another trick in my presentation folder bag has been to hire a high school or college art student to letter my pages and paste in the illustrations. Sometimes they've even done original drawings for me. Because he's still a student, the tyro charges less than a professional artist. One high school senior did a 15-page book for me for a flat rate of $75. Other students, who worked on an hourly basis, charged me $4 an hour.

Once you've achieved a nice-looking graphic folder, practice making your presentation with suitable words—basically you'll use an adaptation of the 1-2-3 Magic Package module. One good way to kick off your presentation is to think of your potential customer and a problem he might have that some of your canvas accessories could help solve.

To demonstrate: After a few pleasant preliminaries in his office you could start out with a statement of purpose such as—

1. "Mr. O'Connor, I know you've had some problems protecting loads on your trucks. May I show you how our truck covers solve that problem?"

2. For the middle section of the presentation module you turn the pages of the folder and, guided by headings and subheadings, give specifics of the advantages of your truck covers.

*Talkamatics tip #33: When making your presentation to a customer, show enthusiasm—because it's your enthusiasm and interest coupled with the potent persuasiveness of seeing what he's hearing that will sell your customer. And up your sales records!*

As you wind up, you again make your statement of purpose and ask for the order.

3. "So you see, Mr. O'Connor, our truck covers can save your company loss of money from damaged goods. Since your truck colors are black and red, would you like your covers in black or red?"

**Other uses.** You also can use your graphic folder for making presentations in your club, community and church work. And why not use it within your company, too—in a one-to-one conference about something important, such as switching to a new system that can save the firm money or some possible areas for a new branch location? The see/hear presentation will be stronger than just your verbal presentation. And it can lead to many growth opportunities for you.

## 3. Putting Yourself Across in an In-Company Presentation

A way to attract favorable notice in your company as well as further your career is not only to do a good job making presentations to your boss but also to make outstanding persuasive in-company presentations to others in your company.

When I mention this, possibly you think, "It's not hard to make a persuasive in-company presentation—like presenting a new plan or procedure. So why do I need to read a book about this?"

If you think that's so, you should be at some of the seminars I've attended where everyone from chairman of the board to marketing managers, purchasing agents, salesmen (*salesmen*? yes, salesmen!), accountants, foremen, shipping department supervisors of some of the country's blue-chip firms try to make a simple presentation about a new plan or procedure and bomb out.

And I mean *bomb out*! Horribly. Not only with shaking knees and quavering voices but also with erroneous persuasive presentation planning and thinking. As one executive sitting next to me commented, when the purchasing manager of a large textile corporation finished giving a report, "This guy gives the impression he can't think his way out of a paper bag, much less persuade anyone to accept a new procedure."

Yet I've seen these jello-style word slingers, by following a few simple rules, turn into persuasive presenters with punch and polish.

So let's consider the important how-to's.

**Talkamatics tip #34:**  *If your planning of an in-company presentation has been solid, you're about three-fourths of the way to scoring a home run in presenting.*

In planning, you must kick off by asking yourself the purpose of your presentation. (You'd be surprised how many fiascos occur because presenters don't do this!) So to begin with, think of your *purpose, purpose, purpose*. What is it? Nail it down.

Your purpose might be to:

— Give information
— Explain a plan or procedure
— Make a progress report
— Teach improved methods
— Give a financial report

However, besides your purpose of wishing to, say, give information or explain a procedure, you generally have a sub-purpose: to persuade people to *use* the information or to *adopt* the procedure.

So chisel out clearly in your thought both the purpose and the sub-purpose of your presentation.

**What does my audience know about my subject?** The next step in planning your persuasive presentation is to ask yourself that question. Consider exactly who'll be in your audience. What knowledge, opinions, prejudices will your listeners have about your subject? What else will they need to know about?

If you'll present an improved procedure, think of any prejudices your listeners might have about the plan, or any objections they might raise. To illustrate: Perhaps the procedures will eliminate one job and the other department members will feel resentful about this. If the company plans to transfer this person to another department, include this information in your presentation.

**Collecting facts.** In preparing your in-company presentation, assemble all the facts and information. Then, keeping in mind what your audience needs to know, decide on exactly what you'll include.

**Preparing your presentation.** Follow these success steps:

1. Note each point you plan to make on a 3"x 5" file card.

2. Arrange these points in logical order.

3. Now, again apply your terrific little friend, the 1-2-3 Magic Package module. Choose a compelling opening sentence that has an Other-Person Benefit in it—why this information will help the listener or why a vexing problem can benefit from this solution. In the middle section, give the

points you wish to make, and end up with a restatement of your opening. You may also wish to add a request for action from your listeners—such as their cooperation in putting the procedure into effect by a certain date.

4. Completely familiarize yourself with but don't memorize your presentation. ***Talkamatics tip #35:*** *In a presentation, plan to talk in vivid, everyday language with active, picture-making verbs, few adverbs and adjectives.*

5. Prepare visual aids. See suggestions for making effective ones in Chapter 5.

6. Rehearse thoroughly your presentation, using your visual aids and lively gestures to vitalize your voice and wake up your audience. See Chapter 7 for tips on how to gesture and Chapter 9 on how to project enthusiasm.

7. Time it. A simple presentation shouldn't run over five minutes. ***Talkamatics tip #36:*** *Rarely should any presentation last longer than 20 minutes.*

8. Carefully prepare, in sufficient quantity, any material you plan to give out after your presentation.

9. Anticipate questions that will arise. And make sure you'll be able to answer them satisfactorily. Check Chapter 11 for guides in answering questions effectively.

10. Check out in advance the room where you'll make your presentation. If you're using an easel or lectern see that it is in place, and make sure that there are enough chairs, arranged the way you wish, and paper and ball points if you want your audience to take notes.

**Giving your presentation.** Remember, always talk *with* your listeners, not *at* them. Talk with enthusiasm. Use eye-contact, described in Chapters 9 and 10 on rehearsing and giving a speech.

***Talkamatics tip #37*** *is always use the above checklist for success in preparing your in-company presentation.*

Use these presentation pointers and you'll start to see some marked progress in your career. But then you'll discover a new problem: talking well is more than just persuasively presenting ideas to others. You must *negotiate* skillfully with your boss, co-workers, suppliers and customers. You'll find nifty negotiating tactics in the following chapter.

## Chapter Check-Back

1. *Putting yourself over with the boss:*
- *Asking the purpose of the meeting* with the boss clues you in on what to bring.
- *Reading the mental climate*—whether the boss is relaxed or pressured—helps you to mesh with his mood.
- *Presenting ideas broadly* can be done by using the 1-2-3 Magic Package module.
- *Adding details* to your presentation should be done when your boss requests more information.
- *Leaving a memo* with complete information is a good idea after making a verbal persuasive presentation.
- *Finding when your boss likes you to make oral presentations*—once a week, twice a month or only when something special arises—is a must.
- *Keeping in mind your boss' interests*—for instance, increased company profits, building sales, keeping a lean staff—will help you tie in your presentation more effectively with what he's trying to achieve.

2. *Putting yourself across with a graphic presentation folder:*
- *Making a graphic folder* is simple with supplies—such as an 8½"x 11" folder with plastic-covered pages, colored felt-tip pens, Scotch tape, colored tape—available from a stationery or office supply store.
- *Organizing and "creating" the graphic folder* is done by listing sales points in the best possible order, illustrating these sales points with pictures taken from magazines and catalogs, swatches of materials, using figures and making charts and graphs.

- *Practicing making a presentation* with the graphic folder and then delivering it with enthusiasm to a customer can greatly increase your sales average.

3. *Putting yourself across in an in-company presentation:*
- *Knowing the purpose* of the presentation is the first step in preparing it.
- *Following certain pointers*—collecting available information, knowing what your listeners need to hear, using the 1-2-3 Magic Package module, employing visual aids and gestures—can help achieve an in-company presentation that can powerfully enhance your career.

# Four

# Successful Negotiating with Talkamatics

Do you always see eye to eye with people you work with in business? Do you agree completely with others' ideas, plans, procedures, tactics and strategies?

Probably not. It's often impossible to agree exactly. You usually need to negotiate. The Talkamatics system shows you how to handle verbal fencing easily and successfully.

## Horse Trading Takes Place Constantly

To illustrate: You negotiate with a friend about borrowing his lawn mower, with a prospective employer about job duties and salary, about terms when buying a home, with a friend about when and where you'll go sailing, with your wife about where you'll go to dinner or for your vacation or whether you'll move with her to a new location if she gets a better job or vice-versa.

Negotiating, negotiating, negotiating goes on unceasingly. So you must know *how* to negotiate well beginning with...

## The Cardinal Point of Negotiating

Today, if negotiating is well done, no one comes up a loser.

Royce A. Coffin, in his fascinating book *The Negotiator: A Manual for Winners* (AMACON) says, "Indeed, it's a hallmark of successful negotiators that both sides emerge as winners."

When pact-making goes well, often some scientific swapping techniques undergird it. So let's look at some negotiating do's and don'ts.

## Do Begin Negotiating by Listing Points

In beginning a negotiation, a Talkamatics winner technique is to consider: What points do I wish to gain? Why do I wish to gain them? And how do I gain them?

List these things. For example, if you're a sales manager of an office supplies store, you might wish to negotiate with the manager of the delivery department to get an improved customer delivery system. So your list might read:

1. We need earlier-in-the-day deliveries.

2. We also need delivery to a 50-mile instead of the present 25-mile radius.

3. Would like (not vital) to offer twice-a-week instead of weekly deliveries to some good customers.

4. We need the first two points in order to offer service equal to our competitors.

5. Improved service can bring us increased business and profits.

6. I can gain these points by working out details with Oscar Urley, manager of the delivery department.

7. I must get an okay for the improvements we agree upon from our operational vice president.

Then think about the person you'll deal with. What will be his objections to the points you present? What will he hope to gain in a negotiation? (You can't figure out everything, but make an estimated guess.) How can he gain by negotiating with me? How can I help him reach some of his *other* goals (not just the ones we're negotiating on)?

List all the considerations you can think of from your table-facer's point of view. In the case of the office supplies delivery manager these might include:

1. (His objections to your proposals.) It will take more trucks and drivers to deliver to a 50-mile radius than a 25-mile radius. Will the company okay this added expenditure?

2. (What will he hope to gain in a negotiation with me?) He's been dissatisfied with the delivery forms the salesmen have been filling out and probably will want them redesigned.

3. (How can he gain by negotiating with me?) Oscar probably would like to gain more recognition from management that he is doing a good job, as well as drivers in his department.

4. (How can I help him reach some of his other goals?) Have to watch if these emerge in the negotiation, then see if I can help him reach them.

## Do Employ a Cooling-Off Period

Here's a Talkamatics automatic: Stash your lists in your desk drawer and go about your work. From time to time, think about the points. In several days, go over the list again and make any changes dictated by time's perspective.

*Talkamatics tip #38: However, it's not always possible to draw up lists—your own and your surmise of your opponent's aims—without doing some homework.*

## Do Careful Homework

Sometimes you must collect and read memos and files, consult trade publications, write to your industry association or talk to various people in your organization to have facts at your fingertips.

One show-you: If you wish to work out an improved delivery system some of the salesmen in your department may give you specific instances of how the present system has worked poorly, or a salesman can tell you how a competitor's delivery system out-performed your company's.

*Talkamatics tip #39: In a negotiation, homework often makes the difference between coming out with a bag of goodies or with an empty bag.*

## Do Observe Your Go-No-Farther Boundaries

Before you start to trade off with a co-worker or someone else in a working-together situation, always think over your proposition and decide on your go-no-farther boundaries.

With the delivery negotiation, you may decide you'll concede various things but stand firm (1) that the routes must be reworked to include a 50-mile radius and (2) on obtaining earlier-in-the-day delivery.

## Do Light a Time Fuse

Always go into a meeting with a timetable in mind. For instance, if you wish to get the delivery system overhauled, say it should be done by April 15, the date of the salesmen's meeting. The reason? Then you can announce the new procedures at the meeting and raise sales force morale.

Figure out a definite time by which you need a negotiation concluded. If you don't, the tendency is to talk, talk, talk, and then for the other side to say, "Well, there's no hurry. Let's think about this for a few weeks." And so things drag on and on with no action and much wasted time.

## Don't Overlook Cheerful Surroundings

If you can control the place where you'll talk, use a Talkamatics target-reacher. Opt for a place with pleasant, bright surroundings. If you plan to horse-trade with the delivery manager and his office seems drab, you might make a colored flip chart for your points (see how in Chapter 5).

Also wear a light-colored suit and a bright print tie, or a vivid dress.

Or for your wheeling and dealing you might suggest you talk over a cup of coffee in your company cafeteria, color-splashed with an art exhibit.

**Talkamatics tip #40:** *Studies show that deal-making fares better in an attractive environment. So try to trade in spirit-raising surroundings.*

Also try to place your opponent in surroundings he feels happy with. When I was in the advertising business, the ad agency I worked for acquired a self-made and very rich client. We negotiated with him every quarter to approve the next quarter's media contracts and layouts for magazine and newspaper advertising.

In the first meeting with the "loaded" client, our account executive invited him to a posh lunch at an elegant restaurant. But the client refused the lunch invitation.

The next quarter, when the account executive called on the client with contracts and advertising layouts, he again mentioned lunch. The client shuffled some papers, then said, "Well, I like to go to the corner drug store for lunch."

The A. E. formally invited him to a ham sandwich and a malted milk around the corner; he accepted with tremendous enthusiasm; between bites, he approved the contracts and layouts without a change and said he wouldn't need to see the A. E. till the next quarter. He turned out to be a very inexpensive client to service, one the agency made a lot of money from, and one we could have lost if we hadn't negotiated in the lunch spot he preferred.

## Don't Neglect Ego-Stroking

When you go in to make a deal with someone, always start off with some ego-strokes. Perhaps a comment about his office ("Say, you've moved your desk. Much nicer!") or a hobby ("Notice your tennis racquet. Hear you won a tournament last week!")

## Do Kick Off with a Benefit for the Other Person

As you go from an ego-massaging pleasantry, try to begin the conversation with a potential benefit for the other person, as you learned to do in earlier talk modules. Some how-to-do-its:

(*To the delivery manager.*) "Oscar, I've been meaning to tell you what a good job the salesmen and I think you're doing. We've come up with some ideas for a little revising of our delivery system which, I feel, would make your system function even *more* effectively...."

(*To a club worker.*) "Meredith, I'm hearing from all sides what a good fund-raising chairperson you're making. Now if I suggest some good prospects for contributions...."

## Don't Skip Your Own Interests

For example:

(*To the delivery manager.*) "Oscar, I've been meaning to tell you what a good job the salesmen and I think you're doing. We've come up with some ideas for a little revision of our delivery system which, I feel, would make your system function even *more* effectively...help the salesmen do a better job... and create more profits for the company."

(*To a club worker.*) "Meredith, I'm hearing from all sides what a good fund-raising chairperson you're making. Now if I suggest some good prospects for contributions, maybe you could help me get some of them for new members."

In building these talk bridges, you're showing your table-facer:

1) You expect to negotiate.

2) He (or his department) will receive a definite advantage in the deal-making.

3) You're a reasonable person; you're not looking only for your own gains.

Signalling these things to your opponent establishes a frank, warming atmosphere in which to tee off a negotiation, and can contribute to its success.

## Do Honor the Invisible "I'm Important" Sign

When you negotiate with someone, always remember he wears an invisible "I'm Important" sign. If you're dealing with several people in a meeting, bear in mind that all —the junior as well as the in-charger—sport this label. *Talkamatics tip #41: Treat each person in negotiating as if he's classy, charming and clever.*

## Hints for Dealing with the Decision-Maker

In negotiating with more than one person, always spot the decision-maker. You can often, by questions, find this out before you go into the meeting. If you're not able to check beforehand, usually it's apparent when you sit down. The decision-maker will receive special deference from others in this group. And frequently, he'll sit at the head of the table.

Should he come on as a low-key decision-maker and you can't ferret him out, simply ask who'll make the final decision.

*Talkamatics tip #42: Always direct your remarks to the entire group, looking with good eye contact at each person, but look longest each time at the decision-maker. As his objections begin to surface, pay particular attention to answering them. Once you've convinced him you can successfully button up your deal.*

## 12 Talkamatics Ways to Steer Negotiating

Here are some Talkamatics target-reachers to steer horse trading.

1. *Decide what you'd like to accomplish.* This is done by making your list as described earlier in this chapter. But at the beginning, don't state in detail the things you want to gain in the negotiation. Simply begin with the benefit for the other person and an indication of gain for yourself.

To replay the benefit statement earlier, you might start out, "Oscar, the salesmen and I feel that a little revising of our delivery system could help your department function more effectively...." Probably by the time you say "revising," the delivery manager will be champing to talk about *his* pet ideas for the department. Listen carefully and...

2. *Find out what the other person wants.* This may not be what you want. To illustrate: You may discover the delivery department is dead set on keeping the status quo. Or he may wish to revamp the delivery system, but not according to the sales department's desires. For instance, the delivery top guy may wish to inaugurate a 10-day delivery system for customers.

3. *After listening attentively* (see Chapter 6 for pointers on removing your business ear muffs), *restate your opponent's desire and see if he agrees to your wording.*

4. *Now describe what you desire to gain—and why.* Again, you'll notice, just as you did in earlier situations, you'll use a module of *facts* to logically explain the points you wish to gain. Logic can be highly persuasive. So in the delivery department analogy, here are some persuaders:

a) "Oscar, let's consider the possibility of offering earlier-in-the-day deliveries." (*Logic.*) "Frankly, there's a real need. Some of our customers won't call in their order till the day before their regular delivery. By that time, they're so low on office supplies, they're desperate for early-morning delivery. When we can't oblige, they turn to other firms. It's costing us business."

b) "Another thing, Oscar, industry is moving out in the country. We can sell to many customers beyond the city limits. We need to broaden our delivery from a 25-mile to a 50-mile radius." (*Logic.*) "Last week 20 potential customers outside our present delivery area called in delivery orders and we had to turn them down. And the week before that, 17 potential customers phoned us. We can't afford to miss out on this new business."

5. *Listen closely to your sparring partner's remarks.* As you expected, he may explain that an increase to a 50-mile radius delivery area would require two more trucks and

drivers. He might also reveal some eye-openers you hadn't thought about—for instance, earlier-in-the-day deliveries wouldn't be feasible because his drivers don't wish to start to work earlier. He's suggested it and some drivers threatened to quit.

6. *Seize upon any possible solution the other person mentions.* For instance, while discussing the problem, the delivery whip-cracker might suddenly get a new idea and muse:

"You know, we might offer a 50-mile-radius delivery and only have to add *one* truck and driver. We might swing it if I sent some of the trucks loaded with next-day deliveries home at night with the truck drivers who live far out in the country. These drivers could start making deliveries on their way to work. This cuts some wasted mileage and time...."

7. *Compliment your opponent, whenever he thinks of a good idea.*

8. *Begin to consider what-ifs.* After you both consider obvious ways to accomplish both your goals, begin to think of alternative solutions.

"But what would happen," he might say, grabbing a pencil and pointing to his area wall map, "if I completely revised *all* the routes. It might be we could get by with renting an extra truck only two days a week and hiring a part-time driver."

As you both begin to look at things creatively in a negotiation, various ideas will occur to you.

9. *Continue to consider creative alternatives.* When the person you negotiate with refuses one of your points, see if you can't work out something from another angle. Or if he offers you an advantage that doesn't seem worthwhile to you, though saying no to this, bring up something you would like.

To illustrate: The delivery department manager says, "I'll tell you what we'll do. We won't give you earlier-in-the-morning delivery but I'll concede this: I'll have the drivers carry some extra small office supplies—paper, ballpoints, typewriter ribbons—and have him check with each office manager on his route. If he needs something in this line, our driver will write up and fill the order on the spot."

You know this idea wouldn't go over with the salesmen who work on commission and wish to write *all* orders, but you don't nix the idea bluntly. You counter with: "If you're willing to do that, Oscar, would you be willing to revise your routes so at least our *most important* customers get early morning delivery?" If your opponent nods yes, then say, "Well, I think *that* revision is the one we want...."

10. *Watch your across-the-tabler for body language that tells you what he may think but not say.* Mini case history: He may say, "I like that idea," but fold his arms across his chest and lean back in his chair, away from you. While he maintains he goes for the idea, his folded arms and away-from-you posture signal that he really doesn't welcome the idea.

At certain points in your discussion a flicker of emotion on your opponent's face, a flash of alarm in his eyes, a slight hand gesture of rejection will tattle to you that these are points he's sensitive on. You'll want to pick your way carefully and reassure him on these counts.

Many times, if we become aware of body language, we can figure it out. After all, our cavemen ancestors wigwagged signals and received gesture signals constantly. So *Talkamatics tip #43* is *to keep your antennae out for body language and frame your negotiation tactics to take care of these unspoken comments.*

11. *What to concede.* In negotiating, concede things that matter least to you.

*Talkamatics tip #44: Also in a negotiation concede things that may seem unimportant to you but for some reason seem important to the other side.*

12. *Use the criss-crossing method.* As you work on trade-offs, go back and forth between what you want and what your fellow negotiator wishes. As you concede here and he concedes there, and as creative alternatives occur to both of you, you'll begin to see a nice package emerge. *Talkamatics tip*

***#45*** is *sometimes the creativity of the negotiation means it's becoming even better for all concerned.*

As you iron out differences and come closer together, try these Talkamatics tactics:

a. *Press a psychological advantage.* While logic will often sell a proposition, sometimes a psychological reason will influence your fellow negotiator even more. For instance, the delivery manager may confide that his department doesn't have enough minority workers, and he'd really like to hire a woman driver. Follow up on this advantage.

Say if he'll agree to work out the things you've discussed, when you talk to the vice president you'll emphasize the fact that the delivery department needs to hire another truck and driver, and the driver could be a minority. ***Talkamatics tip #46:*** *A psychological advantage may be just the thing to cause a negotiation to fall into place.*

b. *Don't be afraid to lay down your proposition first.* Sometimes the tendency is to hang back and let the other person lay down the proposition. You may feel by going first you'll concede too much. But it's better negotiating tactics—and makes a more favorable, open impression—to decide in advance how much you can afford to sacrifice and what you must stand pat on. Then lead the way in stating this.

c. *Introduce a new benefit.* Sometimes when you can't seem to finish up a negotiation satisfactorily, try sweetening the pot with a new benefit for your opponent. If you've reached a stalemate with the delivery manager, and you notice he's plastered his office walls with safety and man-hour production awards, as well as pictures taken at the award presentations, you might trade off with:

"Well, Oscar, let me throw this in. I think we can get together. You're doing a good job, and maybe I can help you get the recognition from the brass that you really deserve. Say, a company house organ story—I'd like to talk to the public relations manager about how you've reorganized the delivery department for more effectiveness and greater company profits. *That* framed story would look nice up there on the wall. And not only the brass, but the company branches as well will read it and see what a swell job you're doing."

**Talkamatics tip #47** is *sometimes introducing a new benefit can turn a trending-down negotiation into a triumph.*

d. *Adjourn, if the session stretches out too long.*

## Winding Up a Negotiation

If you come to an agreement, verbally re-cap, then say you'll put it in writing. Insist that *you* do any writing of an agreement. If someone else does it, errors can creep in and cancel out some of the points you've negotiated. Here's an automatic: Always write up the agreement as soon as possible after the meeting.

Should you find you can't conclude a negotiation, say something like, "Well, Oscar, I feel we've talked things over. While we can't come to an agreement, if you should see your way clear to work out route improvements, give me a call. And if I see a way we could iron out some problems, I'll be in touch with you."

Always leave a negotiation on a cordial note.

And even if you fail to strike a deal, don't hesitate to reopen your horse-trading a few weeks later. After thinking over your proposition, sometimes your opponent decides it does have merit. Or sometimes the deal variables change. Perhaps someone leaves his job. Or a new condition in the nation's economy emerges. Any of dozens of things can occur. All of which means you and your table-facer now hold different cards. Don't fail to play them.

However, though you know *how* to reap the most at the trading post, you can't really excel at pact-making until you know the secrets of good attendance at meetings. So onward to the next chapter, for a gold mine of meeting know-hows.

## Chapter Check-Back

- *Negotiating occurs constantly* in your business, club, community and family life. And in good pact-making today both sides must come out as winners.

- *Doing your homework*—consulting files, magazines, industry reports and people who know the subject—helps you negotiate successfully.
- *Listing points you wish to gain*—and ones you *think* your opponent wants—also helps.
- *Choosing cheerful surroundings* can aid in influencing a deal favorably.
- *In opening your remarks* play up a benefit for the other person. Example (to your boss): "If I could spend less time in the office and more time trouble-shooting I'm confident I could step up the department's production."
- *Honoring the invisible "I'm important" sign* everyone wears is an important part of negotiating know-how.
- *Spotting the decision-maker,* usually the one others defer to, and convincing him is a must in a group negotiation.
- *Steering the negotiation* is done by (a) deciding what you want, (b) finding out what the other person wants, (c) reading body language, (d) seizing upon any possible solution the other person offers, and (e) considering creative alternatives.
- *Pressing a psychological advantage,* laying down your proposition first, introducing a new benefit, and setting a time limit are all result-getting tactics.
- *Observing your go-no-farther boundaries* is essential.
- *Writing up the agreement* should be done by you—and as quickly as possible.
- *Winding up a trade-off pleasantly* and reopening deal-making, if necessary, can pay off BIG!

# Five

# Persuasive Talkamatics for Participation in Meetings

Today your career is going nowhere. Tomorrow you skillfully attend a meeting and your career starts upward. And as you expertly take part in other meetings, your career can continue to go UP, UP, UP.

But the questions are: How do you attend meetings adroitly? What are the secrets of preparing for meetings? Observing meeting protocol? Contributing creatively? Using visual aids like a pro?

## Making the Right Things Happen in Meetings

In a meeting, you want to be thrifty with words and generous with bright ideas. What you say and how you say it can take you up the ladder *mucho quicko*. Here are some target-reaching guides that pay off big in meetingland.

1. Always find out in advance the purpose of the meeting.

2. Do your homework—review memos, files, read magazine and house organ articles, and talk to other people for information. Be as well briefed as possible prior to the meeting.

3. When feasible, work out your contributions or solutions to problems early. One show-you: You plan to attend a meeting to consider fund-raising ideas. *In advance*, noodle out a few possibilities.

*Talkamatics tip #48: Plan ahead. Then in the meeting you can easily pull several ideas out of your hip pocket.*

## Being Bright and Brief

Use the 1-2-3 Magic Package module described in Chapter 2 to structure your remarks. This technique will aid you in talking vividly.

A nifty way to achieve brevity is to limit your comments to two or three minutes at one time. The average person talks at about 125 words per minute. Count 375 words in a magazine article, then read them into a tape recorder. Notice how much you can say in about three minutes.

*Talkamatics tip #49: Practice and get used to talking in three-minute time blocks.*

## Tips for Hitting the Target

Never go to a meeting and stay a silent presence. Meetings are *action* occasions. If meetings are a strange territory to you, here's a quick checklist of ways to contribute.

You can (a) ask questions, (b) make an approving or encouraging remark about someone else's contribution, (c) share some information, (d) point out a weakness or danger in a proposed action, (e) throw out a germ of a good idea, and (f) present a new idea or suggestion.

Remember *Talkamatics tip #50: Speak the first few words of your remark in a slightly-louder-than-usual voice to gain others' attention.*

While the above are meat-and-potatoes meeting guides, the following pointers will help put more jingly stuff in your jeans, move you into an office with a view, and make you a hero or heroine in your business, club or community work.

**Early-bird timing.** Find out the meeting agenda and decide when you'll offer your remarks.

*Talkamatics tip #51: In most meetings never delay offering your ideas.*

Funny things can happen in meetings. While you remain modest and mute, someone speaks up and voices the idea you planned to present. Or meeting time runs out before you give your idea. All bad news for you. Why? Because the put-outers get the raises and promotions.

**Test ideas.** When you prepare ideas to offer in meetings, test them. For example, for a general department meeting, conceivably you may have half a dozen things you could talk about, so which do you choose? First of all, choose workable ideas. Iron out the kinks. Check with other people until you're sure your brain babies will make sense. Then, in addition, where practical I like to give meeting ideas the "5% Profit Test."

Imagine you have an arrangement with the company which gives you 5% of the profits. Naturally, this makes you profit gung-ho.

So when you go to a company brainstorming meeting to improve your company's profitability, instead of suggesting a unique, expensive Christmas party idea to build employee morale (let the potential career drop-outs do that), throw out some names of potential customers (which you have carefully researched) whose business the company could go after, or ways to reduce costs, or get more done in less time.

Try to specialize in presenting time-saving, efficiency-improving, problem-solving, business-building, profit-making and other ideas of that ilk.

*Talkamatics tip #52: You advance fast if you make "profitable" contributions in meetings.*

**Innovative ideas.** When you do your homework, usually you find several ideas occurring to you to present. Which ones should you choose to offer at the meeting? The Talkamatics rule of thumb: Other things, such as profitability or workability, being equal, choose the *innovative* idea.

People thirst for the new and different. And if it's not feasible to present an entirely innovative idea, often you can give an existent idea a fresh twist.

Here's how: Your club has broken money-raising records for several years with its flapjack breakfast. When discussing this year's fund-raising event, naturally don't suggest abandoning a money-tree like the flapjack wingding. But don't suggest another flapjack spree that's a carbon copy of last year's. Suggest an innovation—for example, holding it adjacent to a petting zoo where the kids can play with the animals.

*Talkamatics tip #53: Presenting innovative ideas (if workable, profitable) can draw attention favorably to you in meetings and help you ascend, ascend, ascend in your career or club.*

## Pointers for Chairing a Meeting

If you attend meetings like a pro, making valuable contributions, you'll receive an opportunity to become chairperson of a committee. And if you do a good job, you'll become chairperson of another committee. And another! And chairing meetings can lead to exciting breakthroughs in advancing your career and your extra-curricular activities.

You'll want your chairperson duties to turn out super well. So here are 10 pointers for persuasive chairing that lead to LEADERSHIP. (Talkamatics rates these as automatics to follow.)

Locale. Always advance-check on the meeting room to see (a) that it's suitable, and (b) whether you need to rearrange, alter or add anything.

One vigilant chairperson always conferred with the restaurant manager about the meeting room every time his club met. Each time the manager noted with approval the room read-out and the intelligent changes the chairperson requested. After the fourth session, the manager offered the group a room twice as big and far superior to the first room, without increasing the price. Why? The manager said, "I've noticed you people are particular and appreciate good arrangements."

Extra care. Check out the props, visual aids, working microphone and lectern, and see that pencils and pads are in place.

Agenda. A typical agenda might run:

- Calling the meeting to order.
- Reading of minutes of last meeting (asking for additions and/or corrections).
- Old business (often this means unfinished business).
- New business (new motions, proposals, ideas).
- Adjourning of meeting.

*Talkamatics tip #54: A survey of 200 successful meeting chairpersons showed that an agenda was a chairperson's most powerful and persuasive tool.*\*

"The important thing," says one meeting chairperson, "is first to *write* out your agenda, and then *hold* to it. By carefully weighing what will be on the agenda, then writing it out, you avoid non-essentials, but you don't neglect anything important. By sticking to your agenda you keep the meeting from getting off the track.

"Quite often people in meetings bring up things at the wrong time. When corrections are asked for in the minutes, someone may bring up a new proposal and want to talk about it. So as an alert chairperson, you must constantly orchestrate discussions and re-slot subjects to the proper place."

A for-instance: When Henry Evans asks an irrelevant question, you might say, "Henry, let's stay with the subject we're on. When we've finished, you can bring that up."

Never waste others' time. Practice directness, economy of words. Generally, give information, handle business, present a speaker in the most direct way—and you'll rate as a great meeting presider.

---

\*Chamber of Commerce of the United States, *Highway to Successful Committee Meetings* (Washington, D.C.), p. 6.

*Talkamatics tip #55:* *A tightly run meeting displays the chairperson's expertise. Often one hour is the maximum desirable time for a meeting.*

**Details.** Handled well, details can help make your meeting a hit. A show-you-what-I-mean? Okay. One meeting chairperson carefully slotted only one minute each for sales talks by various individuals at a company sales meeting.

The participants were rehearsed so their talklets stated one sales problem and one solution—for instance, one type of customer resistance and one solution to this customer resistance.

Such detail manicuring helped make the event a tremendous success.

**Equality.** To preside capably, you must enforce equality. Note the "horns and halo" section a little later in this chapter.

**Revealer.** Often as an in-control meeting presider you must skillfully bring out the opinions of the shy or unself-confident people. One trick a with-it chairperson utilizes is to familiarize himself with the backgrounds of people attending his meeting. He then can say, "Well, John, you're an accountant. How do you feel about this financial plan?" Or, "Diane, you worked for a printing company before joining our firm. What kind of job jackets did they use?"

**Spotlight.** A meeting maestro, whenever appropriate, plays the spotlight on as many accomplishments of others as possible. But he shines the spotlight briefly, so as not to bore others.

**Helps.** A knowledgeable retail store manager holds popular sales meetings because he schedules plenty of persuasive "helps" to his employees in meetings. For example, one meeting might demonstrate product features the sales personnel could use to make more sales. Meeting attendees always appreciate helps for their business, interests or hobbies, and the chairperson who schedules such helps.

_Intrigue. *How* you say things when you're in charge can captivate or bore an audience. **Talkamatics tip #56: *If you're a live-wire meeting major domo, you'll watch your language: weed out cliches; avoid verbosity; use colorful verbs.***

An able presider may add short, fresh, humorous, pertinent remarks or interesting anecdotes, preferably *after* handling the meetings musts.

_Power. By doing the above things a chairperson can preside with power and persuasiveness. He'll prove Michelangelo's statement, "Trifles make perfection, but perfection is no trifle."

**Talkamatics tip #57** is *perfecting your chairperson skills is a way to go up the ladder pronto.*

## Avoiding Horns and Halo

In a meeting, beware of pinning on anybody one of two labels:

1) Horns
2) Halo

**Horns.** Sometimes in a group session, people will try to make one person a bad guy. For example, you attend a meeting to, say, present a new traffic plan to a group. A Skeptical Sam may speak up and point out the plan's flaws. Immediately you may detect a negative group reaction to Sam—as if he's wearing *horns.*

Don't let this happen. Quickly start guiding Sam with your questions so he'll bring out his points more clearly. Sometimes Skeptical Sam is right, and something in the plan can be improved. If Sam's all wet, you can help the group reject his objections in a friendly way. The meeting will remain harmonious and you can go on to other things.

**Talkamatics tip #58:** *Never allow a group to pin horns on anyone.*

**Halo.** Also you should strive not to put a halo on anyone in a meeting. Of course, give praise where due. If someone comes up with a great idea, or performs excellently, comment warmly on his feat. But don't place a halo on his head.

Too-effusive praise embarrasses the person receiving it. Also over-praise may make the other people feel uncomfortable and insecure—that they *lack* the abilities or accomplishments of the halo-ed person.

## Staying Alert for Five Types of Meeting Birds

At meetings, you must stay alert for five types of meeting birds. Once you spot these, and know how to feed and care for them, the meetings you participate in can turn into winners. The first two meeting birds are *positive* types.

**1. The Wise Owl.** In most meetings, you'll find at least one person who by reason of good judgment or experience behaves and speaks with marked wisdom.

Often you can spot him by such characteristics as: (a) careful listening, (b) faculty of seeing all sides of a question, (c) ability to foresee things that might occur, and (d) more interest in seeing that the right course of action for all prevails, rather than actions which would benefit only him or his department.

Support the Wise Owl. Always help him bring out factors the group should know about. If you serve as chairperson, appoint the Wise Owl to the most important committee work.

**2. The Eagerling.** Here's another positive type of meeting bird to give TLC—tender loving care.

You'll recognize the Eagerling by his eagerness and enthusiasm for a meeting or committee to accomplish great things. The Eagerling's eyes may sparkle, he's energetic and willing to do the work of two or three other members, and will strive for real attainments. The Eagerling often exhibits imagination.

The Eagerling's weakness may lie in lack of experience and practicality. Either guide the Eagerling so his efforts will produce desirable results or team him with the Wise Owl.

The next three birds possess *negative* characteristics which you can turn into plus ones.

**3. The Ostrich.** This bird buries his head in a meeting. Ask him his views and he declines to say, for fear of committing himself before he knows what will be the popular view.

You can peg an Ostrich by (a) his desire not to speak out, (b) his lack of decisiveness for either side of a question, (c) his fearful air that declaring himself for or against something might hurt him.

In dealing with an Ostrich, keep asking his opinion on things about which he has specialized knowledge. Pretty soon, as his confidence grows, he'll state his opinion on meeting issues.

**4. The Colorful Commando.** This highly intelligent bird often sees ideas, routes to take, and solutions far faster than others in the meeting. He often sports a big ego ruff and likes to run things.

Before you know it, the Colorful Commando can take over and run a meeting—unless you block him.

If he starts to dictate a course of action, simply say, "Ralph, we want to get some *group* thinking. I need everyone's viewpoint before we act."

If you refuse to let him take over the meeting, often he'll fall into line and put his energies behind the group decisions. Sometimes, however, he'll find an excuse to leave the meeting early—and eventually drop out of the group altogether.

**5. The Spotted Downbeat.** This bird has a whiney-complaining chirp. But usually about *small* things.

Psychologists tell me the Spotted Downbeat is someone who feels *unloved*; thus he finds fault with things and others. If a Spotted Downbeat starts his negative notes, he can soon get the other meeting people singing a negative song, too.

So stifle the Spotted Downbeat quickly. Should he chirp about the air conditioning? Point out a warmer spot he can move to. No sugar for his coffee? Offer him a saccharine tablet or ask someone to get him sugar.

Then, whenever possible, follow up with a compliment that will help him feel more self-confident or loved. Example: After he deplores the air conditioning, you might comment, "You're looking very fit today, Arthur."

I once saw the board chairman of a large ad agency become a momentarily unloved Spotted Downbeat in a Plans Board meeting. He presented some campaign ideas which didn't turn on the other committee members. Suddenly overcome with emotion, the chairman rushed out of the meeting.

The president of the company overtook him at the elevator, threw his arm around his shoulder and said, "We all like your ideas, Milt. We were just quietly considering them. Why, we all *love* you, Milt." In the most loving way, the president led Milt back into the room and Milt ceased to be a Spotted Downbeat and was soon once again the Wise Owl of the meeting.

A little loving care and the Spotted Downbeat will forget his negativism and become a productive meeting member.

## Checklist for Meeting Marksmanship

Every so often, the Talkamatics system advises going down this checklist for hitting your target in meetings. Keep checking your progress so flab doesn't hinder your meeting marksmanship.

— Do I attend at least 70% of the meetings I should?

— If I can't attend at least 70%, do I see if I can shift my schedule so I can either improve my batting average or not have to attend these meetings?

— Do I get to most meetings a few minutes before they begin?

— Whenever possible, do I know the purpose of the meetings and do my homework so I can contribute?

— Do I take only committee assignments I can give proper time to?

— Am I mentally and vocally active in a meeting? Contributing ideas, suggestions, remarks?

— Do I work for the common good of the meeting, and not merely for my own interests?

— Do I handle the meeting birds mentioned above wisely?

— Do I refuse to be wordy, impatient, time-wasting, or bring in unrelated matters?

— Do I *enjoy* working in a meeting?

Score yourself 10 points for every Yes answer. A score of 80 is good, 90 excellent, and 100—well, you're *talking* your way up the ladder!

## Types of Sophisticated Meetings

As you move upward, you'll attend various meetings. Through the years these have become more sophisticated. So it's often helpful to learn their types and how to take part in them.

**Small-group meetings.** These are held in the office of your company, client or supplier. Attending—any number from two to about 15.

Some rules: Be businesslike. If you're an attendant, be sure you make brief and pertinent remarks. If you're in charge, don't let a small meeting run two or three hours (as it frequently does). Don't go to an outside meeting—at a client's office, for example—and overstay.

Small meetings utilize input from everyone attending. In speaking in small meetings, you can be more personal, using names of the other people frequently, referring to their interests and knowledge of a subject.

*Talkamatics tip #59: You must listen completely in a small meeting. Never "turn off" after you've made your presentation or remark.*

**Clinic.** A briefing/training/educational meeting (on subjects varying from small-business budgeting to salesmanship techniques) for people actively working in the field to gain the latest knowledge. Usually 20 attendants or less. Some tips for attending: Think ahead. Take any materials you wish analyzed. Plan in advance questions you'd like answered.

**Workshop.** Resembles clinic but less emphasis on instruction and more discussion by participants. Usually gives practical solutions to group problems by specialists in the field. Frequently limited to 25-35 people.

**Conference.** Conference attendants talk about a subject or related subjects under the guidance of one or more experts. Frequently much discussion. Object: Often to solve a pertinent problem of considerable concern to the group. Generally limited to 15-20 conferees, and a one-to three-day schedule. In attending a conference, read as much background material on the subject as possible.

*Talkamatics tip #60: Identify the type of meeting and use the pointers in this book to attend successfully.*

## Employing Effective Modern Illustrations

Today in meetings you often must use visual aids. Without a doubt, the training of military personnel during World War II proved the worth of audio-visual materials. Experiments with many people from varying environments and educational background showed that *visual* input accounted for 85% of learning.

When visual aids were added to verbal presentations, instructors found people could soak up 35% more knowledge in the same length of time. The results were exciting. There was a 55% better retention of information.

Since then, the use of visual aids has soared.*

The Talkamatics system teaches there are two parts to every talk: (1) the spoken words, and (2) the visual impression.

As you know, part of the visual impression you make is through your appearance, your expressions and your gestures. The other part is through the skilled use of persuasive visual aids.

Talkamatics is not only bullish on visual aids, but advises, as **Talkamatics tip #61:** *Use persuasive visual aids whenever and wherever possible.*

## The Potent Flipper You Can Make Yourself

One of my former bosses in a large ad agency rated as one of the most persuasive presenters I ever saw. His secret weapon? A large paper flip pad on which he roughed out with his felt tip marker words, figures and charts he wanted his clients to remember.

Many a time he won a new account for the agency or "saved" a wavering one by going to a client's office with his flip chart and making a presentation.

You too can experience great results with a flip pad you make yourself. What's more, you'll find creating a flip pad surprisingly easy.

## Suggestions for Making and Using a Flip Pad

You'll recall in Chapter 3 you learned to design a graphics presentation folder for a one-to-one presentation.

*Stephen S. Price, Business Ideas: *How to Create and Present Them* (New York, N.Y., Harper & Row Publishers, 1967), p. 172.

Now, for audiences up to 50 people, you can employ this basic technique to make a flip pad. Use a large white heavy paper pad. A good size is 30″ x 40″.

**Design.** Keep all points briefed as much as possible. (These main points are described in detail in Chapter 8.) Make main point lettering at least 3″ high, subpoint lettering at least 2″ high.

**Illustrations.** Be sure illustrations are simple enough to be quickly understood and BIG ENOUGH to be seen easily.

What if you want to show a detail on a car? For example, a headlight? Show only the detail, not the whole car, in a blown-up photo.

Freehand drawings, even if they're simple, can be effective.

*Talkamatics tip #62: Don't worry if your drawings look like kindergarteners' rejects. Oddly enough, no matter how crude, your drawings will get your point across in a fresh, spontaneous, audience-appealing way.*

And *Talkamatics tip #63: Another advantage to do-it-yourself illustrations is your flip pad doesn't look too slick and expensive. Often it's desirable in business today to appear as if you don't throw money around on production.*

**Showmanship.** When lettering your flip pad with a marker, here's a Talkamatics target-reacher. Omit a few important words or figures. Merely pencil them in lightly. Then in the presentation, with a flourish write in these words with your marker. By doing this, you emphasize your points and snap up your presentation.

*Talkamatics tip #64: You can also dramatically complete a drawing on the spot by going over lightly penciled lines.*

To remind you of points, names or figures you want to mention, jot these lightly in pencil in the lower corner of your flip pad. Presto—you'll have a built-in prompter!

*Talkamatics tip #65: Be so familiar with your talk and flip pad, you can point to your flip pad while talking directly to your audience.* Never turn and face your flip pad and talk to *it*!

It's best to keep your flip pad covered till you use it! Then people won't start examining it ahead of time and tuning out what you say.

## Developing Thrifty Illustration Cards

Consider asking a professional artist to make illustrative cards (basically your flip pad presentation in more permanent form) which you can use for an easel presentation. Ask him to cut costs wherever possible by using thrifty Prestype (an inexpensive type many printers have).

A card presentation looks professional. If you plan to deliver this presentation a number of times, cards will wear longer than a paper flip pad. Also you can rearrange cards and vary your presentation. *Talkamatics tip #66: To control costs, always work out the finalized card copy before giving it to an artist.*

## The Adroit Slide Show

What happens when you show visual materials you can't put on a flip pad? Or when traveling? The Talkamatics system advises putting your presentation on 35 mm slides and using a projector. Heeding these automatics can help you attain a persuasive performance:

1. Show all your slides at one time. Then you won't keep flicking the room light on and off, distracting your audience.

2. Make sure the quality of slides is good—edit out any blurred or poorly posed ones.

3. Get a nice variety of slides. You can even buy or borrow a few to flesh out the ones you own. (See Chapter 12 for where and how.) Adding a few first-rate slides will give a new flair to your presentation.

Another way to zip up your presentation: If you wish to show a business advertisement, memo or magazine article that's mostly type, mount this material on brightly colored cardboard, then make slides, and the result will be pleasing in your slide show.

4. Use certain slide tricks. Remember how a TV show or a film adds interest by certain cinema tricks—for instance, going from a far shot, to a medium shot, to a close-up of a building or persons, or reversing this order? Do the same thing with *your* slides. If you want to show an environment problem, make one slide an overall view of a factory with a chimney pouring forth smoke, the next slide a medium close-up of the factory and chimney, and the third slide a close-up with billows of smoke coming from the chimney.

## If You Use Professional Artwork

1. *Seek professional help early.* Allow at least six weeks to three months to prepare visual aids. Good work takes time.

2. *Fill in the pro with all necessary information*—what the visual aids will be used for, where, your objectives. The better the background briefing, the better job he can do.

3. *Always get a written estimate of costs* before you give the go-ahead for professional visualizing.

4. *Finalize all basic concepts and wording,* including slide or film scripts, and get written okays from the necessary people in your company before giving the written copy to the designer or advertising agency. ***Talkamatics tip #67: Making changes after any visual work has been completed can cost plenty, while making changes in typed form costs peanuts.***

Now, while you have the basic know-how to handle meeting bugaboos like a pro, something else is needed. It's how to strip off your hidden earmuffs in business situations. The next chapter will give you the Talkamatics techniques to listen straight up the ladder.

## Chapter Check-Back

- *Pre-meeting maneuvers* include doing home work—reviewing memos, files, magazine articles and talking to other people for background information.
- *Being bright and brief.* Use the 1-2-3 Magic Package module to structure, edit, and keep your remarks vivid. Try not to talk more than three minutes at a time.
- *Contributing in every meeting is vital.* Do this by (a) asking questions, (b) making an approving or encouraging remark, (c) sharing information, (d) presenting the germ of an idea, or (e) presenting a new idea or suggestion.
- *Offering your remarks* in a meeting should generally be done *promptly.* Delay means someone else may express—and get credit for — ideas you want to present.
- *Judging ideas by the "5% Profit Test."* Imagine you'll get 5% of the company's profits. This will mean you'll strive to present ideas and information that build business, save money, increase efficiency, and improve profits. And thus you'll set yourself up to receive bonuses.
- *Chairing a meeting with professionalism* is done by writing out your agenda, editing out unnecessary (and if possible, boring or dull) items, then sticking to your agenda. Often one hour is the maximum desirable time for a meeting.
- *Acting as a meeting maestro includes fair and equal treatment* to all attendants. Avoid pinning horns or halo on anyone. Spotlight the accomplishments of as many of the members as possible.
- *Staying alert for these five meeting birds* is advisable: (1) The Wise Owl—experienced, interested in right

course of action for all. (2) The Eagerling—
enthusiastic but lacks practical experience. Team
with Wise Owl. (3) The Ostrich—won't speak out pro
or con. Tame by asking his opinions where he has
special knowledge. (4) The Colorful Commando—big
ego ruff. Don't let him take over. Get the opinions and
input of all. (5) The Spotted Downbeat—negative
about small things. Praise him and he'll chirp
positively.

- *Employing visual aids* greatly helps your audience to
stay attentive and retain material.
- *Using a flip pad persuasively* can make a zipless
speaker seem zippy.
- *Showing slides expertly* can help your presentation
zing. Display good-quality slides. Rehearse with the
projectionist. Talk loud enough over the slides to be
heard. Run all your slides at one time. Don't be a
lights jockey—turning lights on and off for slides.
- *Using an expert designer*, if your budget's ample, can
turn a presentation from well-planned into...WOW!

# Six

# The Talkamatics Way
# to Very Persuasive Listening

There is one important secret every top salesman discovers. As he learns to be a more effective *listener*, he becomes a more effective *talker*, and he advances his career.

You, too, can advance in your career by better listening.

However, an article in a sales magazine* cites some troubling statistics. Research studies under controlled conditions show that most people have a mere 25% listening ability. Also, in conversations a salesman and his prospect tend to remember less than 50% of what the other was saying.

Yet, it is pointed out, many top-compensated salesmen and successful people in the country's giant corporations have studied how to listen, and use attentive listening to help them succeed.

How do you boost attentiveness? How do you listen successfully? What are the tips and techniques? This chapter will give you ideas on areas where it's advantageous to listen acutely, as well as rules to improve your hearing. Let's begin with...

## Listening Up the Ladder

Listening well can further your career.

Fresh out of college, Frank Venton joined a Wisconsin optical manufacturing company. One day he asked a

---

*Winfield C. Hanson, "Through Artful Listening," *The American Salesman*, October, 1968.

secretary why she spent her lunch hour typing business letters, and listened carefully to her reply.

"Oh, I *have* to work during lunch," she said. "We're flooded with letters asking about the company's products. I can't finish my work unless I work during the noon hour."

Frank asked if he could read a batch of letters. In a short time he returned with a number of form letters he'd devised, permitting the secretary to handle this type of correspondence rapidly. The procedure saved the company thousands of dollars.

This innovation, along with others he suggested, helped earn promotions for Frank, who went on to become president, chairman of the board and, later, United States Senator from his state.

Another superb listener I know, Rick Clark of Greenwich, Connecticut, always tried out new products for youngsters—for which he was to prepare advertising copy—on his own kids. He listened carefully to their reactions. Then he incorporated the reasons why they liked these products into persuasive radio and TV commercials. This tactic earned him awards for good work, and juicy promotions.

So **Talkamatics tip #68** is *by talking with others and listening attentively to them, you can rise in business.*

## The Art of Boss-Listening

One situation where you often need to employ acute hearmanship is when you listen to your boss.

Numerous case histories indicate employees often fail to listen with concentration to the guy who runs the show and don't accurately get information from him. They hinder their careers because they don't understand what the boss says or wants.

Here are some musts to remember when conferring with the head man:

**Clarifying through close listening.** Even if the person you report to speaks poorly, your being "all ears" will help him speak more *understandably.*

**Talkamatics tip #69:** *Psychologists say "hard" or intent listening makes a person talk more clearly and phrase his points more precisely.*

Also, if you listen with full attention, you can easily ask for clarification, if needed.

**Listening for what the boss ranks as vital.** This may seem simplistic, yet many employees continue to overlook this. In conferring with your boss, stay alert for what he rates as vital for you to do right away. Possibly it may seem insignificant compared to other things you're handling. However, generally a company quarterback can see the large picture better and knows what requires priority. Assure him firmly you'll handle it pronto—and do it!

**Talkamatics tip #70** is *alert listening—detecting your boss' priority, telling him you'll take care of a task post-haste, and doing so—can help you sprint up the corporate ladder.*

**Listening to solve short deadlines.** When asked by your boss to do a job with a too-short deadline, listening and responding persuasively can often get you off the hook.

When your boss confronts you with a mini timetable, answer something like: "Sure sounds exciting. This can lead to a big contract. But let's go over again what you said, so I'll have all the details."

As your boss talks, you'll hear portions of the assignment you judge he'll need earlier than other parts. When your boss finishes, say, "I think I get the picture. Let's consider the timetable. Wouldn't you say the first thing I should have ready is (*name it*)?" You listen to his answer. Then ask, "And by about (*naming a date*)?" Again, you listen to his reply. "And after that, don't you feel I should concentrate on...?" And so you continue listening, questioning, listening, questioning till you pin him down to a suitable timetable.

Notice, you're drawing forth a module of facts from the head guy. When you listen-question expertly, you prevent the person you're talking to from (1) not giving you enough facts and (2) drowning you in a river of unconcrete words.

## Listening to Enlist Others' Help

Should you plunge in and ask someone's help when you need to get things done in your work and projects? Before asking for someone's helping hand, it's often better, first, to listen skillfully to learn his background and then ponder how you can utilize it.

Moving to Jacksonville, Florida, Liz Levy joined a community club. "I was appointed chairperson of a committee," recalled Liz, "to operate a booth at shopping centers to give out literature and answer questions about the club. Before lassoing committee members, I asked questions, listened and learned various people's backgrounds and talents."

She then invited a professional newspaper reporter, two professional artists and a maintenance person who worked for a large bank to form the committee. Intrigued because she offered them posts in line with their abilities, they accepted.

She soon had the artists making signs and designing an arresting portable booth. The maintenance man borrowed, with his boss' approval, one of the bank's large maintenance trucks to transport the booth and materials to various shopping centers. And the newpaperman publicized, with good coverage, the club's tie-in to local events.

The outcome? Many people visited the booth. The club membership grew. And committee chairperson Liz Levy also received the offer of a desirable full-time job, managing a retail store for another club member who noted her ability.

*Talkamatics tip #71: By listening to learn others' background, often you can expertly utilize their experience to contribute to a project's success.*

## Influencing Others

How do you influence others to cooperate with you in your work and community projects? One target-reaching technique is not to flat out ask for their cooperation. Instead, lay a foundation of listening.

Find out *their* interests or needs. Then you can direct your talk specifically to that need—often with exciting business results.

A friend of mine, Nick Hanson, wanted to attract more customers to his Idaho chain of surplus stores.

In conversations with people at gas stations, restaurants, drugstores, supermarkets and the newspaper where he ran his ads, he began to lighten up on his own talking and heavy up on his listening.

He found they desired denim jeans, all styles; camping gear; hunting and fishing equipment; and boots and other footware.

Nick then revamped his advertising. He designed brief slice-of-life commercials, with the man on the street saying what he'd like to buy and Nick, as owner, answering and describing his large stock of these items. It was a most effective device, and Nick recorded the biggest profit year in his business history.

**Talkamatics tip #72** is *if you want to influence others, tune in on what concerns them. By aiming your efforts to meet their needs, you'll work with them far more effectively.*

## How Uncritical Listening Pays Big Dividends

One day, when George Tollman was director of personnel for an Ohio bedding company, he talked with a man who'd gone on the warpath against his boss. "He's an egomaniac, impatient, gives hard-to-understand instructions. I'm fed up," said the employee. "I'm quitting."

George asked the man to first try what he calls uncritical listening. "Listen closely and sympathethically— *uncritically*—to everything your boss says." The result? Before long, the employee left the warpath, became a valued, harmonious employee and received a raise.

"In fact, I've noted many times," said George, "when someone is having difficulties on his job, if he'll listen with perfect attentiveness and sympathetic interest to his boss, he'll succeed."

When you listen uncritically to others, they feel relaxed and liked. And they like *you*.

A successful interviewer on a TV book review show is known for his uncritical critic's approach to interviewing authors about new books.

He persuasively conveys, with sympathetic nods, chuckles and smiles, his admiration. The authors respond by relaxing—and performing well. The result is that the critic hosts a highly popular show.

*Talkamatics tip #73: Uncritical listening can help make many good things happen for you.*

## Becoming Listener-Centered

A secret of good listening is becoming listener-centered. Here are some helps for doing so:

1. *Sit up and listen.* The advice, "Sit back and listen" is poor. Leaning slightly forward, in a comfortable but alert position, helps you listen more efficiently.

2. *Don't allow distractions.* The best target-reacher way to listen to someone is to keep your eyes on him. If you glance around the room, you cut your attentiveness and won't remember as much of what he says.

Always cut out other distractions, too—by closing a door, turning off a background radio, and moving closer to the speaker whenever possible.

When speaking on the telephone, it's wise not to look at papers in front of you or study a picture on the wall. Instead, either look at a blank wall, stare into space or form a mental picture of the person you talk to. You'll hear far more of the conversation.

3. *Curb thought-wandering.* Because many people talk at about 125 words a minute, and you listen at a rate of about 500 words a minute, your thought outraces a talker. What happens? Your thought gallops along—considering your job, a movie you'd like to see, and whether to buy some new sports

equipment. And this thought-wandering may cause you to miss parts of conversations that could greatly help your career.

So how do you whoa-down your thinking? One trick: consider what points the talker may make next. If he tells you about a problem in the service area of his business, rivet your thought on this subject. Speculate mentally that this may mean some changes in manpower, in services rendered, in the amount of time employees will work.

Then keep alert to see if he touches on those points. **Talkamatics tip #74:** *If you keep your thought subject-centered, instead of self-centered, you'll really hear conversations. In fact, by listening expertly, you'll become a more persuasive talker and your whole career will blossom and grow.*

## Listening for the Important Unsaid

Another valuable technique you can master is to listen for the unsaid. Sometimes the unsaid is more pertinent than the said.

A steel company business manager, Paul Jans of Pittsburgh, saw his organization's profits suddenly plunge due to a recession. Paul carefully tightened his department's belt, but didn't slash personnel.

He explained this strategy in monthly meetings with the corporate vice president to whom he reported. After several months, Paul became aware in a meeting that the corporate VP was not asking about his strategy but about Paul's No. 2 man. Was he happy? Was he well rewarded?

Paul knew he had treated No. 2 well. Later, analyzing the conversation he realized the important *unsaid* was that the corporate VP probably was planning to oust him and promote his No. 2 to his job.

My friend did some checking and found his No. 2 was undermining him, his decisions and implementation. Quietly, my friend arranged for No. 2 to go on longer and longer business trips, and also requested him to re-do some unsatisfactory work.

Before long, the ambitious No. 2, on his own, quit. In a few months, industry sales were up and my friend Paul's department was showing a nice profit. My friend found management once again giving him bravos and bonuses. "But I wouldn't be sitting here today if I hadn't been alert to what was unsaid, as well as said, in my monthly meetings," noted Paul.

So **Talkamatics tip #75** is *listen not only for everything that's said in a conversation, but also for the important unsaid. Figure out what's missing and act accordingly.*

## Four Guides for Taking Off Invisible Ear Muffs

While you may agree that you can solve many talking problems by correct listening, you may say, "But it's difficult to listen intently. I'm not naturally a good listener."

Obviously, with the noises and distractions today, many of us don't hear as acutely as we might. At various times we wear invisible ear muffs. Yet we can remedy lack of attention. Here are some pointers to help you remove your ear plugs:

**1. Have one-minute practice-listening sessions.** One minute of every hour, advises Dr. Ralph G. Nichols, formerly head of the University of Minnesota's Department of Rhetoric and a foremost listening authority, give your fullest attention to listening to something or someone. It might be a six-year-old child, or a cricket, or an airplane passing overhead, or a snatch of music.

**Talkamatics tip #76:** *In that minute of listening, forget yourself and your problems. Really listen. Don't be critical.* Don't think about whether you like the music or whether the six-year-old talks well for his age. Simply listen. And hear *everything* during that minute. This isn't easy to do, but it will greatly improve your listening.

**2. Listen for the main points.** In every conversation what is important for you to remember are the main points someone makes, and any subpoints that support these main points. Anecdotes, for example, are trimming, and you needn't remember these.

*Talkamatics tip #77: As you listen attentively, try to isolate and remember the pertinent points.* You then have this information in your memory bank to use later.

*Retention exercise:* For several days, while hearing various radio talks, try jotting down the main points and subpoints supporting the primary points. Then later, after conversations with friends, do the same thing. Before long, you'll find you retain the meat of what's said and discard the fat. You then can talk persuasively to the main points.

**3. Don't react emotionally.** Another target-reacher for removing invisible ear muffs: Keep your emotions in check when listening. Don't react emotionally—even if you hear something disturbing—until you hear the speaker out. I've known listeners to get their adrenalin flowing when they hear words like "cutback," "taxes," "riots," and "leftist."

An emotional listener might even conclude that someone, say, was advocating more taxes when in reality, if the person continued to listen, he'd discover the speaker's views were against increased taxation. *Talkamatics tip #78: Much misinformation and wrong action springs from emotional listening.*

**4. Listen with thoughtful interest.** The fabulous career of TV star Art Linkletter proves that listening well pays off. In his fine book *How to Be a Super Salesman,* Art describes how he listens when he interviews on a TV show.

> I suppose one key to my success as an interviewer in radio and TV has been sympathetic, encouraging, thoughtful listening. Some interviewers, instead of thinking about what their guest is saying, spend the time

thinking up a wisecrack or another question. So their interview goes nowhere...

When you don't listen to the other fellow, don't seem interested in him, he resents it and may hold it against you.*

## Getting a "Fix" on a Situation

As you ascend the executive stairs, there are times you may need to know more details about a situation or the significance of something. The fastest way to get this information often is by listening.

When I went to Charlotte, North Carolina, to head up an in-house advertising agency for a real estate firm, I found there were things I needed to know for the smooth running of the agency. And I must know them fast!

Fortunately, my door was always open to staff, and in a few days I found that by *listening* I was getting fixes on situations. One example: Our account supervisor every so often would drop into a chair, ostensibly to smoke a cigarette and chat, but then she'd mention an advertising job going through. "How's it working out?" I'd ask.

"Oh, all right," she'd answer, "but why don't you talk to the art director?" or "the production manager?" I soon learned when she mentioned people it wasn't idle chat, and to get with them, and find out the problem. By listening carefully for even a slight hint of smoke, I would learn of difficulties which I could quickly iron out.

*Talkamatics tip #79: Often you can get a helpful reading of a situation just by alert listening...then you'll know what to say.*

## Probing for the Solution Kernel

In any business or club discussion, when two or more people get together to talk, often it's about a provoking problem.

---

*Art Linkletter, *How to Be a Supersalesman,* ©1974. Published by Prentice-Hall, Inc., Englewood Cliffs, N.J.

You can save much effort if during such a talk you listen carefully to what's voiced, because often the solution kernel lies in what is said right in the meeting.

Former President Eisenhower, noted as an excellent listener, often probed for a possible answer when an aide briefed him about a troubling situation. Eisenhower would say, "How's that again?" or "Will you clarify that?" When the aide did so, frequently in the re-telling the solution occurred either to him or to Eisenhower.

## The Talkamatics Methods of Taming Your Tongue

The Talkamatics system of listening includes taming your tongue by these methods:

*First:* If you're like most people, it's better for you to speak less and put more meat into your talk. In other words, use the Talkamatics 1-2-3 Magic Package module given earlier in this book to structure your remarks.

*Second:* Hear the other person out. Even if it takes a few minutes longer, listen to all he wishes to say. Often you receive surprising light on a point when you let a person talk without starting tongue action yourself.

*Third:* A workable way to tame your tongue is to judge after someone speaks. We all tend to make quick judgments—based on appearance or the manner in which a person handles himself. Listen and judge *afterward.*
**Talkamatics tip #80:** *Many people make a mistake in judging others, talk too soon, break in, challenge the speaker or change the subject—and miss out on important remarks.*

A friend of mine, Robin Neff, once received a big job by taming her tongue. At a giant Midwestern conglomerate, she worked in a divisional PR capacity. In the elevator one day she met an executive who headed up the marketing activities of another division.

He asked her if she knew anybody who could handle his divisional publicity. Robin was approaching her floor and she started to say, "Sorry, afraid not!" and jump off. But instead she curbed her tongue, got off the elevator with him, stood listening, realized the job was a super one, and ended up taking it herself.

## How to Steer While Listening

A good listener by his facial expression—for example, a slightly baffled look at something he doesn't understand, or a quickened look of interest at something intriguing—can help make even a poor talker talk better.

Also, an adroit listener can ask appropriate questions to help steer conversations to make them clearer. What questions should you ask?

## Five Questions to Ask

The newspaper reporter answers in a news story the five questions: *who? what? where? when? why?* Often in a business conversation, you'll find you need to ask one or two of these questions for clarity's sake.

I personally like to hold back on my questions as long as possible in a business conversation. My thought is, "Get the other person talking." As he begins to slow down, I insert my questions. I find this often gives me more knowledge of a subject than if I appear to come in quickly with questions and grill the other person.

## The Say-It-Back Technique

Another mark of a pro listener in a business situation is the use of the say-it-back technique. To illustrate:

When you receive instructions from someone, it's wise to say back briefly what you heard to make sure you caught everything.

A manager assigned to launch a new product for a manufacturing company was given carte blanche to draw the best people from several departments to help him. He found, however, under the pressure of their new assignment, they often didn't hear exactly what was said. For instance, if he asked for something in three days, it wouldn't appear. Checking, he'd find the person thought he'd said three weeks.

However, one executive always rephrased what he assumed were the manager's main points. Everyone noted how efficiently he was functioning by replaying what was said. Later, no one was surprised when he became one of the fastest risers in the company.

You can solve problems by astute listening and talking. In fact, 20-20 listening will help you to polish your talking ability. But Talkamatics has still another wonder worker to aid you in becoming a persuasive speaker. This fun-and-wonder worker is *gesturing*. Find out how to employ body language in the next chapter.

## Chapter Check-Back

• *Listening attentively*—for example, becoming aware of needs in your business—often reveals worthwhile opportunities to pursue.

• *Listening closely to your boss* tends to cause him to talk more clearly, clarify his meaning and phrase his points more precisely.

• *Hearing what the boss thinks is vital for you to do* often can help you move ahead.

• *Tuning in for what matters to others,* their wants, interests, goals is essential if you wish to influence people. By helping other people obtain what they need or want, you often can reach your own goals.

• *Listening uncritically* to others helps them feel relaxed and liked. And they like *you*.

• *Becoming listener-centered* means (1) sitting up and listening, (2) cutting off distractions, such as closing a door and (3) curbing thought-wandering—anticipating what the speaker will say next, instead of thinking about your personal concerns.

• *Keeping an ear cocked for the important unsaid* is advisable. In a business situation, you may discover that someone fails to touch on an expected matter, then says something seemingly unrelated. By analyzing his remarks, often you become aware of an unsaid, puzzle out why it was left unsaid, and solve a business problem before it becomes too serious.

• *Taking off invisible ear muffs* can be done by (a) one-minute practice-listening sessions—concentrating completely on, say, a child's chatter or music; (b) becoming alert for the main points of what someone's saying—for instance, the anecdotes are trimming; (c) not reacting emotionally—judging *after* the speaker has talked; and (d) listening with thoughtful interest.

• *Getting a fix on a situation,* becoming alerted to possible trouble, is often accomplished by being "all ears" when someone chats with you.

• *Looking for a solution to a problem?* Many times keen listening helps provide an answer. During briefings former President Eisenhower, an excellent listener, many times would ask an aide to repeat something or clarify it. When the aide did so, frequently the solution to a vexing situation occurred to him or to Eisenhower.

• *Steering conversations* to bring out necessary points. You can do so by your facial expression—and questions about who, what, where, when, why.

• *Using the say-it-back technique,* repeating briefly what someone's said, then pausing and *listening* will often help you correctly understand your boss' job directions.

# Seven

# Persuasive Gestures
# That Reinforce Talkamatics

When that expert speaker, evangelist Billy Graham, spoke before a record-breaking crowd in Korea, his Korean interpreter stood right beside him. However, the interpreter didn't just stand there. As six-footer Billy gestured with strong, emphatic, endlessly varied gestures, his short interpreter gestured exactly as Billy did.

When Billy leaned forward confidentially toward his audience, the interpreter leaned forward. As the twosome moved, pointed, gestured in unison, the smooth performance not only indicated a lot of previous practice but also that to get across points today you must *use body language*. Even if you're an interpreter!

Once Barbara Walters, then co-anchorwoman of TV's *Today Show*, leaned forward to interview a guest. When asking a question, she pointed to him and then to herself, as she said, "Well, don't you and I feel...." Later she made an expressive "out there" gesture to indicate midland United States. And a little later her hands circled in bewilderment to explain she wanted something clarified. On and on, during the show, she punctuated her talk with interesting visual movements. It added up to a professional performance.

## Gestures Make You an Instant Professional

Without a doubt, the quickest way to pump pro technique into your talking is with telling gestures. Body language helps you (a) explain the points you make; (b) underscore their importance; (c) give visual movement, so you don't look boring, even frozen; (d) keep your audience's attention; and (e) visually reinforce your words so your audience better remembers what you say.

*Talkamatics tip #81: And one super reason for gesturing is it cuts much of the tension and nervousness you feel in talking.*

In fact, I like to tell talkers that employing body language lets you stay loose as a goose—a good position from which to talk effectively.

## Gestures Spark a Dud into a Dynamo

At a speaking seminar in New York I watched middle and top executives go from average talking to good, and some even to very good status, via intensive drilling in gesture-talking. Hour after hour, instructors coached these business people on body language: "Don't just gesture with your right hand...bring that left hand up! You're still using too much right-hand movement. Bring that left into play...*left*... LEFT!"

The instructor continued: "So you kick off your talk with a little anecdote about your golf game. You describe a putt. Put your hands on that imaginary club, tap the ball, make your listeners *see* that play...and you'll have a lot more fun yourself, and relax, too."

To a business woman: "All right, you wish to describe a call on a big-shot client. He's got a tremendous circular desk? A tall, knock-out sculpture on the coffee table? *Then get your hands moving*! Indicate that desk with a big circular motion..make that a really *big* circle....Now show that tall sculpture with your hands. *Show* your listeners. Make that piece TALL. Get your hands apart. Make that piece *taller*...I said TALLER!"

As the execs followed these directions they began to emerge as persuasive speakers and not bores.

*Talkamatics tip #82: Lively gestures help you sound vivid and interesting.*

## Helping Hand

When I worked for a large advertising agency, I saw an example of a competent advertising person—I repeat, "competent," not genius—who ladder-climbed to the top. Ron Schultz, a small-town boy turned big-city copywriter, was a hungry, hard-working, good thinker, with profit-making ideas. But so were some of the agency's other people.

But a difference with Ron was his way of punctuating his talk via helping-hand gestures. In a knowledgeable way, he used the helping-hand gestures you'll find in this chapter that lead to talking well in business. He rose from copywriter to supervisor to creative director to president of the agency.

And you, too, can employ these helpful gestures on your daily job.

## The Daily-Job Gestures for Fast Success

Here's some non-verbal language that helps you move ahead in your career.

1. *Pointing.* In business, use the technique of pointing to things—to a wall map, a bar graph, a section of a report—to make your talking more *understandable.*

You can also point to ideas—for example, before you as you talk about a plan your company uses right now and behind you to show a plan your department used several years ago but has since discarded.

2. *Separating.* Many times in conversing with someone you need to make certain things clear. Use a separating motion with your hands. To illustrate:

If you say, "On the one hand, we can adopt this procedure..." put your hands over to your left. When you say, "On the other hand, we could try this procedure..." shift your hands over to your right. The points you make will stand out separately.

3. *Holding up various fingers when enumerating* is an especially strong form of hand gesturing that should be added

to your gesture portfolio. For instance, if you say, "I'd like to make *three* points," hold up three fingers. Then when you say, "First," raise your index finger; "Now my *second* point," let your middle finger join your index finger; and so on.

Do a lot of enumerating, both in your daily conversation and talking with groups. Enumerating indicates you won't ramble or digress. After you talk, business associates can recall the signposted points you made.

*Talkamatics tip #83: Signposting—holding up corresponding fingers when you enumerate points, reasons, ideas, etc.—is a great way to give your talking clarity and visual appeal.*

And *Talkamatics tip #84: Business rewards people who SIGNPOST.*

Since it's estimated over 95% of our gestures are with our hands, there are many other daily-job actions you can utilize. But don't just use intellectual ones...also use *friendly* gestures.

4. *The friendly gestures.* In your daily job you can make many of these friendly gestures—ranging from a warm hand salute when you meet someone to extending your eye-contact to *everyone* when talking in a meeting. Here are two categories of "friendly" body language to emphasize:

• *The interested-in-others body language.* Two illustrations: (a) the welcoming pulling out of a chair when someone comes by your desk or into your office to talk; and (b) attentive head-nodding as you listen, indicating you understand and are interested in what someone is telling you.

• *Approval body language.* You'll find many actions that signal, "I approve of and like you." One: making a circle with your thumb and forefinger to show a co-worker he's done a standout job.

I remember Ron Schultz, referred to earlier, stopping to inspect some advertising layouts an art director, Dennis Larsen, stayed up until 11 p.m. the night before to finish.

When Ron saw the excellent layouts, he clapped the A.D. on the back and expressed his pleasure. The A.D. flushed with delight and was eager to get back to his drawing board and complete the other layouts for the assignment.

Naturally, you begin to converse more expertly when you use friendly, interested-in-others, approval body talk. And your reputation as a vital speaker will grow whether you speak with your boss, a member of the opposite sex, Mr. or Mrs. Big in the community, or someone of another generation.

***Talkamatics tip #85*** *is gestures can help you cement solid relationships with others.*

## Making Them Larger Than Life

In videotape replays of business talkers, it's clear that many people, when employing body language, use too-small, too-tired-out gestures. This annoys the person you talk with almost as much as if you speak too softly. To gesture well, most people should make larger, firmer, more energetic gestures than they customarily do.

For example, gesturing with your hands? Let the movement also include your arms and shoulders. Never make a "hands only" gesture. It looks feeble and weak-wristed, and gives the impression you lack enough redblood cells.

***Talkamatics tip #86:*** *The larger your group of listeners, the larger your gestures should be.*

And remember ***Talkamatics tip #87:*** *In delivering a talk before a group, keep your gestures high—above your waist—so everyone can see them.*

Along about now you may say to yourself, "I didn't know hand/arm gesturing had so much to it. I wonder if I've been doing it wrong. How *exactly* should I use hand action?"

The following three-step description for a hand/arm gesture will show you how to do it correctly and avoid the milktoast "hands only" gestures which lack heft and energy.

1. *Getting ready.* Your hands get in position to make the gesture. For example, you bring your hands up before your chest prior to describing a large circular desk.

2. *Accomplishment.* You make the gesture. For instance, you describe a large circle with your hands and arms.

3. *Return.* Your hands return to your side—the best launching position for your next gesture.

*Talkamatics tip #88: In speaking before a group, when not gesturing, always keep your hands relaxed at your sides.*

You'll gesture more effectively from this position than if you must untangle arms folded across your chest, or hands clasped behind your back. If you deliver a lectern talk, you can either keep your hands at your sides or rest them lightly on the lectern.

*Talkamatics tip #89: Don't lean heavily on a lectern or desk.*

## Assuming the Action Posture

To gesture effectively, adopt the Talkamatics action posture. Essentially, this means pulling in your abdomen, holding your chest high and out, your back straight. This applies both when standing and sitting.

Another reason for the action posture is that when you gesture properly with your hands, you actually gesture with your entire body. Your ankles, legs, torso, head should be "behind" that gesture. The action posture allows this.

## Four Techniques to Successful Gestures

Here are four techniques to successful gesturing:

**1. Make positive, confident gestures.** Always try to put some heft behind your gestures, as described in the previous section. Next time you tune in on a local TV news show and catch an interviewer talking with a business person about a charity drive or commenting on the economic scene, notice his gestures. Wouldn't they be more effective if he moved his hands more positively? Made larger gestures than just weak-wristed ones?

*Talkamatics tip #90: By working before your mirror, you can develop interesting self-assured gestures.*

**2. Match gestures to words.** A foreman wished to indicate that morale had become high in his newly organized section. However, he moved his hand feebly when talking to his boss. His boss remained convinced the foreman was covering up something, that morale wasn't high.

Since morale *was* good, the foreman should have indicated this by pointing confidently upward as he talked about morale. He should have said, "I *repeat*—morale's real high..." and pointed his finger even higher to the ceiling.

*Talkamatics tip #91: For effective gesture-talking, match your gestures to what's said.*

Also, time your gestures to occur on the part of the sentence you wish to emphasize. One how-it's-done: If you talk about how your company will hold personnel at a branch location to 250 employees and write this figure on a blackboard, chalk in the figures at the same time you say them.

*Talkamatics tip #92: If you use corresponding body language at the same time you say an important phrase, you'll greatly strengthen your talking.*

**3. Use varied gestures.** Whether it's everyday conversation or speaking to a business group, employ a nice mix of gestures: both hands in unison; each hand singly; some other body language such as a shrug or an absorbed leaning forward; some head movements and expressions that go along with your words and reinforce them appropriately.

*Talkamatics tip #93: You'll note the above is a gesture module—built on a Talkamatics principle. The principle? Variety! Never neglect variety in gesturing.*

Keep mentally monitoring your body language. Ask yourself: "Am I merely repeating the same gestures all the time? How can I bring some variety into my body movements?"

**4. Gesture to vitalize your voice.** A problem with many business people is a lusterless, unpersuasive voice.

Walt Gilbert, a TV director in Tucson, Arizona, said, "While you can study with vocal coaches and make a big deal out of correcting an unvital voice, an instant voice strengthener is to gesture.

"As you gesture with interest," said Walt, "your voice becomes more interesting. In fact, tape yourself talking for about five minutes without gesturing. Then repeat that message with vigorous gestures and notice how your voice tends to grow more dynamic with gesturing. An animated gesture will help make a person's voice sound *enthusiastic,* too," said Walt. "And in business I've found enthusiastic guys and gals don't finish last."

## How to Invent the Right Gestures

While in speaking you often employ gestures that others do (example: using your hand like a meat-cleaver to make a point forcefully), probably some of the best gestures you utilize are the ones you invent.

But you may wonder, "How do I invent persuasive gestures?"

This is not hard to do. In fact, it's one of the most fascinating aspects of the Talkamatics system. Here's how to play gesture-inventor:

a) Observe, study and "adapt" for your personal life-style the best of your friends' gestures. By drawing from your observation of your family, friends and co-workers, and adapting some of the best gestures to suit your delivery, you soon develop a number of fresh gestures.

b) Turn off the sound and watch actors on TV. You'll see many gestures you can "borrow" for your own speaking. When you attend movies and plays or listen to other speakers, every so often shut out what they say and concentrate on their gestures. You'll discover some beautiful body language you can re-tailor for your own use.

c) Play the "tape-ape" game. Tape a dramatic sequence from TV which features an actor of your own sex. As you tape, note and count his gestures, from cocking his head to rising from a chair. Then replay the tape and try to do similar gestures. Next play the tape again, with less "aping" on your part, and see how many original gestures occur to you. You'll be delightfully surprised!

d) On a bus ride or when you visit a shopping center, study people's movements and jot down a few notes to remind you of ways you can gesture for force and variety.

e) When planning a presentation, sit down with pencil and paper. As you think through what you'll say, jot down some appropriate gestures.

With forethought you can become imaginative and inventive in gesturing. Case in point: A real estate man plans to talk of the advantages of a planned housing development. He can speak of the monotonous streets with box-like houses in an unplanned development by indicating a long unbroken path with his hands and using his fingers to draw some boxes in the air.

Then he can speak of the planned development's eye-pleasing cul de sacs by making a large circling gesture with a hand, and show gently rolling hills with an undulating gesture. As his hands go up to indicate tall trees and high rise buildings, his audience's interest will also rise.

f) Rework your presentation so you can develop more compelling gestures. Often as you sit scheming gestures, you realize if you state something more colorfully or concretely, it'll provide a springboard for a lively gesture.

A how-to: You're talking to salesmen about a new product your company is going to give the salesmen to sell. Your first sentence is, "With this great new product, we can increase sales." But you want to make a strong affirmative gesture so you rework your statement to, "With this great new product we can build sales—I mean really BUILD SALES!" You make a gesture as if you were piling up building blocks with your hands.

**Talkamatics tip #94:** *A good gesture can greatly intensify the impact of the benefit you discuss.*

## Controlling Dancing Feet

When business people, club members, church workers and educators talk to even a small group, often the most annoying gesture they make is a little dance.

These dances vary from the omnipresent Sway (side-to-side movement, weight on one foot and then on the other), to the Rock (back and forth, weight on heels then on toes), to the Shuffle (moving feet back and forth as if polishing the floor) and the Beginning Ballerina, in which they rise up and down on their toes. Women execs often throw in a Trembling Knees routine.

The remedy for dancing feet? Think of sandbagging. Stand with your weight distributed evenly on both feet. Then picture a sandbag lying across them. Tell yourself you can't possibly move your feet (unless you need to assume a different position or move to a new location). **Talkamatics tip #95: *Once you get a mental picture of your feet sandbagged to one spot, your feet jitters disappear.***

Other no-no gestures include rattling things in your pocket, stroking your chin, tugging on your ear or fiddling with an earring. Watch yourself in a mirror, get critiques from your family or friends, and get rid of drive-your-listeners-nuts gestures

## Using Powerful Body Language

The Talkamatics system divides sign language into three basic types: realistic, abstract-idea and forceful gestures.

**1. Realistic.** These gestures refer to physical objects. A salesman, talking about the paint job on a car, pats the finish. A football coach holds up a football and shows a neophyte how to grip it. Both are realistic gestures.

**2. Abstract-idea.** This type of gesture describes an abstract or emotional idea. These gestures enforce concepts you can't see with the physical eye. A chemist tells his boss how his department labored and still hasn't come up with a formula for a new kind of shampoo. He makes a sweeping, abstract-idea gesture with his hands.

**3. Forceful.** These gestures describe degrees of feeling such as joy, or worry. For example, if a club president wishes to announce the success of a fund drive, he might announce, "We made our first goal of $500 right on schedule, then we hit $800 by the middle of May. And by our closing next month, we predict we'll reach...$1,000!" Each time he mentions a figure his gestures become progressively more forceful.

Think how dull he would sound if he merely got up and read in a monotone, "So far we've collected $800 and a month from now we expect to get $200 more."

## The Negotiating Gestures That Win Friends

Whether you merely meet with someone in your office to iron out which of you will handle certain parts of a project, or you do some actual negotiating—for example, a new plant space—utilizing the following gestures can help you win friends. And your negotiations go better!

1. Begin the negotiation with a pleasantry and a smile.

2. Put warmth into your eyes during the meeting. Be sure you don't allow a bored, "cold fish," disbelieving or distrustful look. Such eye impressions can help stalemate the negotiation.

3. When listening to the other person's views, don't sit with your arms folded across your chest. This position symbolizes resistance.

4. Listen with interest. A good gesture for conveying this is with chin resting on your hand, and an absorbed look. Nod every so often to show that you comprehend the points the other person makes, and find them well-taken.

5. If you wish to indicate your willingness to cooperate, lean forward as you chat with your across-the-tabler. Rest your weight on the balls of your feet, raising heels slightly.

*Talkamatics tip #96: These gestures will show your friendliness and cooperativeness, help the negotiation come to a more successful conclusion—and in shorter order!*

## How Many Gestures Should You Make?

Each presentation shapes up differently. But let me give you some idea of how much gesturing is going on today. In a study made of 200 TV commercials, the thirty-second commercials contained from nine to 11 gestures and the sixty-second ones averaged 21 gestures. Admittedly, many of these gestures were small, a frown, a slight nod, but they are gestures.

In making TV feature films, a rule is, "If something doesn't move every seven seconds, the audience moves— away from the TV set."

While you won't want to gesture too frequently, remember people today are accustomed to gestures. They want visual messages. *Talkamatics tip #97: It's extremely difficult for the gestureless talker to keep a listener's attention.*

## What If You Prefer Not to Gesture?

Every so often a business person protests, "Well, I really prefer not to gesture. It's not my style." When this happens the Talkamatics system asks, "What happened to the business people who said, 'I really prefer to keep manufacturing buggy whips. Accessories for autos are not my style.' " You see, in gesturing it's not so much what you want to do, but what your listeners expect you to do—and do capably.

## Can You Make Too Many Movements?

Can you over-gesture? This rarely happens with business people. In planning a talk before a small group, it's a good idea to rehearse using more gestures than you need in your final presentation. But during your actual talk, you probably won't recall all these gestures and so will use the right number.

*Talkamatics tip #98: If you're one of the very, very few who come on too strong with gestures, you'll generally see this in your listener's facial reactions. Then you can quickly tone down your actions.*

In making presentations, while you'll plan some of your gestures, stay loose, and use spontaneous gestures when they occur to you. Generally when an urge comes over you to gesture to emphasize or explain a point, do so. If the idea occurs to you to include actions, it probably means a gesture will fit in well.

## Keeping Your Gesture File

So important has visual emphasis become that Talkamatics now advises this automatic: Keep a gesture file to spark your ideas for body language.

Whenever you spot a new gesture you like on TV, or in a business presentation, or made by a friend or relative, make a note of it in your pocket notebook. Later transfer it to a 3"x 5" file card in your gesture file.

Here's an example of a file-card note: "Executive talks with small, informal group of factory supervisors in shirt sleeves. Good gestures: Exec takes off jacket, unbuttons shirt collar, loosens tie. Puts foot on chair, leans forward informally with arm resting on knee as he talks."

Your card file will provide a module of gestures you can adapt and use effectively for many occasions. So every time you plan a presentation, review your body language file for ideas. By privately practicing, you can publicly "toss off" the right gestures, and polish your talking to new luster and liveliness.

But no matter with what liveliness you gesture and speak in every day situations, the time comes when you must give the Big Talk. And you wonder: How do I plan a striking talk?

What can a non-pro talker like me say that'll inform, persuade, convince, interest, intrigue, entertain, amuse, fascinate and satisfy today's smart and demanding audience?

In short, you ponder how you can put together a talk that'll make you sound like a tiger instead of a jolly St. Bernard.

Speech architecture is not difficult if you follow the easy-do speech-drafting techniques in the next chapter.

## Chapter Check-Back

• *Adding body language* can help make you an instant professional at talking.

• *Using body and facial movements* helps attract your listeners' attention, cements their interest, and visually reinforces what's said for more clarity and memorability.

• *Relieving tension and vitalizing your voice* are other big benefits of body talk.

• *Helping-hand gestures* include pointing to things (wall maps, graphs, etc.)—separating points you wish to make by moving your hands—and signposting (enumerating points by holding up your fingers to correspond to the points, reasons, ideas you'll make).

• *Employing daily-job success hand action*—such as pulling out a chair for someone entering your office, making a circle with thumb and forefinger to show a co-worker he's done a standout job—can help you go up the ladder.

• *Making larger-than-life gestures*—in other words, using larger, firmer, more full-bodied gestures than you normally do—can energize your talking.

• *Delivering a hand/arm gesture* consists of three parts: (1) *getting ready*—bringing up your arms and hands to the spot where you'll make a gesture: for example, in front of your chest; (2) *accomplishment*—making the gesture, such as describing a circle; and (3) *return*—your hands return to your sides.

• *Keeping your hands relaxed at your sides,* when you speak before a small group, is the best position to launch your gestures.

• *Pro-style gesturing* includes making positive, confident gestures; matching gestures to words—for example, writing a figure on a blackboard as you say the figure; and using a nice mix of gestures—hands, body and facial movements.

• *Inventing body language?* You observe, study, and adapt the best gestures made by friends, TV actors, people you see on the bus and in shopping centers. In making a talk, plan your gestures with pencil and paper and even re-work your presentation so you can use more and better sign language.

• *Controlling dancing feet* is done by mentally picturing a sandbag lying across your feet so you can't move them.

• *Keeping your gesture file*—noting an effective gesture on a 3"x 5" card—is an aid to successful speaking.

# Eight

# Easy-Do Speech Drafting
# with Talkamatics

One day some industrialists were gathered around a table discussing how they could raise money to build a new college library.

Finally, after rejecting a number of proposed ideas, the head of a large group of department stores said, "I've solved problems in my stores with this little reminder,

'Taken by the yard
Work is hard;
Taken by the inch
Work's a cinch.'

"Why don't we apply the 'inch' principle to this problem? Instead of looking for several big donations, let's look for a lot of 'inch' ones—ask one person to donate money for a chair, another a door, another a roof...."

The industrialists followed this idea and quickly raised plenty of funds.

The "inch" principle can be applied to many situations, including planning a talk. Here's the first inch to consider in drafting a talk.

## Choosing a Winner Subject

To draft a successful speech, you must choose a good subject. But what's a winner? *Talkamatics tip #99* is *a*

*winner subject is one you know a lot about and feel
enthusiastic about.*

Recently I saw the difference enthusiasm can make,
when a Japanese-born junior executive gave two talks at a
speech seminar.

In his first talk, despite his heavy Japanese accent, he
did a creditable, but unexciting, job of talking about
marketing challenges.

In his second speech, he talked on his hot hobby, "Collecting Stamps for Profit." He explained that with $25 you
can start collecting, and your collection can increase in value.
He talked glowingly, and the audience glowed right back at
him because his speech sparkled with first-hand, helpful information. The result? At the finish of his speech the
audience gave him a standing ovation; and then crowded
around him at the seminar break for more information about
stamp collecting.

So whenever you can, choose not only a subject you know
well, but one you feel extremely enthusiastic about. Some
subjects when *you* choose might be:

- Your hobby
- Your work
- A cause that you want to promote (such as helping
  ghetto kids)
- An interesting trip you've made.

Quite often, though, you're asked to talk on a specific
subject, chosen by a group. The Kiwanis Club, for example,
may ask you to talk about how to curb inflation. You're not
an expert on the subject. What should you do? Talk about the
subject anyway, using a *Reader's Digest* article to give you
some facts? Not at all, according to a leading speaker, who's
also written speeches for presidents and governors.

This speaking ace advises you to flatly refuse to talk on a
subject about which you don't have considerable personal
knowledge. Instead, suggest to the Kiwanis Club you'll talk
on your pet interest, jogging.

However, in business speaking, it's not always possible to bring in a new subject in place of a suggested one. A target-reacher alternative is to quickly take a suggested speech subject and shape it to your abilities.

## How to Shape Your Subject

How does shaping your subject work? Well, one day the phone rings and a friendly voice says:

"Mike Williams? This is Ray Biederman of the Distribution Club, and I read in the newspaper you've been promoted to be the company's new general manager and have moved to Centerville. Welcome! You know the Distribution Club certainly would like to have you speak to us at our November 4 meeting. About what? Oh, something about real estate trends...."

Or a memo arrives in the mail with an invitation to speak at a company meeting. The memo says:

"Mike, we read the story in the company house organ on some ideas your department has worked out. It sounds like something all the company's managers should know about. We're having a managers' meeting June 10-11 and we'd like you to be on the program...and give us some details."

Notice, each of these suggested topics, "real estate trends" and "department ideas," is a broad, unfocused subject. ***Talkamatics tip #100: You can shape an assigned indefinite, or even a definite, subject so that you can handle it easily and intrigue your listeners.***

For example, the week I joined Boise Cascade, a Fortune 200 company, as publicity manager for the building products division, a civic group asked me to speak about the publicity problems I encountered with this giant division.

At this point I wasn't into my job at all, so I decided to shape the subject to one I could handle. Since they seemed interested in a "publicity" topic, I persuasively countered with a proposal to talk about a couple of interesting publicity assignments I'd handled in past jobs. They accepted this subject.

And since I would speak after dinner, I felt my talk should be light and humorous. So I chose several amusing incidents that had occurred and also showed some slides of beautiful homes I'd publicized.

The speech was easy to prepare, earned much laughter and applause, and resulted in several letters going to Boise Cascade's president, thanking him for letting me speak.

So jump at the chance to shape a subject to one you can handle. However, whether you work with a subject of your own choosing or one that is assigned to you, **Talkamatics tip #101** is *begin your speech planning with an audience size-up sheet.*

## Audience Size-Up Sheet

If you want to give a speech that'll have your audience vigorously applauding, you must get complete information about your speech setting and audience. You'll need to know everything, from who'll greet you on arrival, to your audience content.

The Talkamatics size-up sheet (see Figure 1) lets you get this information. A Talkamatics automatic: As soon as you accept an invitation to speak, make a photocopy of the ASUS and fill it in.

Even if your secretary or a speech writer assists you with preparing your speech, make sure they fill in the ASUS—and use it in preparing for your speech. Even one gap in your audience analysis can mean trouble.

I recall one busy executive who spoke to a large meeting of clubwomen. He hadn't been briefed on his audience content and he'd just come from greeting a group of wives of his company managers.

Still thinking about the managers' wives, quickly he began to talk to the clubwomen, throwing out pointers on how a wife can help advance her husband's career. Just as quickly a frosty reaction came back from the audience.

Feigning a scratchy throat, he grabbed a glass of water and conferred with the program chairman. She informed him the club's 175 membership was made up mostly of unmarried

(When you accept a speech engagement, ask the program chairman to fill you in on the following details about your audience. Then select a subject that'll interest this type of group.)

1. Content of audience:

   Name of group _____

   Occupations _____

   Sex_____ Age range_____ Number_____

   Educational background _____

   Income level _____

   Political leanings _____

   Religious leanings _____

   What could I compliment them on? _____

2. Proposed subject:

   What does the audience already know about my subject?

   _____

   What do they want to know most from me about this subject?

   _____

   What "cautions" should I take with this subject for this audience?_____

   Would the subject I'm thinking about interest my audi-
   ience _____ Very much?_____ Mildly? _____ Not at all?

   _____

3. Speech checklist:

   Place of speech_____

   Date_____Time_____Length of my speech_____

   Program chairman's name and phone number_____

   _____

   Other speakers on program and subjects _____

   _____

   Person to contact to arrange for showing of slides and microphone use_____

   Person to ask for when I arrive_____

   How many minutes ahead of time can I arrive to check my equipment and talk with projectionist_____

   **Figure 1: AUDIENCE SIZE-UP SHEET**

career women. They couldn't care less about his help-your-husband hints. So he rapidly switched to hints on how his audience could go up the ladder. But his listeners remained chilly. And he said later that he felt he alienated some of his company's best customers.

**Talkamatics tip #102:** *In drafting a speech, use your secret weapon—the filled-out ASUS.*

## How to Employ the "Speed" Factor

Right now, let's consider a vital ingredient in Talkamatics easy-do speech drafting. A Talkamatics automatic is to force yourself to draft your speech *speedily* and *early*.

The first few days after you accept a speech invitation you should:

a) Choose your subject;
b) Fill in your audience size-up sheet;
c) Then outline your topic, according to the following tips in this chapter.

But remember **Talkamatics tip #103:** *Draft your speech with stop-watch rapidity and then you'll have time for result-ful rehearsing.* So now, gallop along in your speech drafting.

## Focusing on Your Speech Angle

After you complete your ASUS, zero in on the persuasive focus or angle of your speech. Basically you want to reduce a big general subject to a focus or angle that's small enough to handle in a speech. You must make sure, also, that this focus is extremely appealing to your specific audience.

While you probably won't have much of a problem reducing a subject to speech-size (that is, you wouldn't try to talk about the rise and fall of civilization in a 15-minute speech), you may have a considerable problem determining if your speech has a lot of audience appeal.

How do you determine this? Well, you shift gears from thinking about yourself and the things you'd like to say to thinking about what Edward J. Hegarty in his excellent book *Red-Hot Public Speaking* (Prentice-Hall, Inc.) calls the M.I.P., that "most important person" in any speech you'll give: your listener. **Talkamatics tip #104: *You want your speech to have maximum "you" appeal for your listeners.***

In determining the importance of *you* appeal in a sales presentation, a popular verse by an unknown author puts it well:

> "So tell me quick and tell me true
> Or else, my friend, to hell with you:
> Less—how this product came to be
> More—what the damn thing does for me."

Not just a persuasive sales presentation, but any speech you give should be loaded with *you* appeal.

Here's how Mike Williams, the general manager of a real estate development spoken of earlier, focused on an angle of a subject so it sparkled with *you* appeal and became absorbing to his listeners.

The program chairman asked Williams to talk about real estate trends.

Williams' audience size-up sheet profiled the club membership, numbering about 60, as family people, in the 35-50 age bracket, and highly mobile. Every few years many of these distribution executives were transferred out of town and other executives brought in.

The mobility factor, Williams felt, gave him an opportunity to tell the executives about the new purchase plan his company was involved in but had not yet advertised.

The plan, in effect throughout the country, was this: A family could pick out a home, live in it on a six-month trial basis, making no down payments, paying a monthly rent equivalent to mortgage payments. If the family liked the home, they could buy it and the earlier rent payments would be applied to the mortgage. If the home wasn't satisfactory, the family could move out with no more obligation than if they'd rented an apartment.

Quite rightfully, Wlliams felt that focusing his speech on this new plan would interest his audience far more than the subject, "Real Estate Trends." But how does Williams or anyone insure he *stays* in the focus of his speech?

## The Working Title

Here's an automatic: To insure keeping to your focus, after you choose your subject, quickly give it a "working" title that spells out what the subject's about. Williams selected "A New Home-Buying Plan for Mobile Executives." Later on he'll brief and shape up his title.

Other examples of a working title:

• An office manager was asked to give a talk to a group of supervisors on maintaining an attractive office environment. She decided to give her subject the working title of "How You Can Decorate Thriftily by Leasing Plants."

• A PR man accepted an invitation to talk to his city's Citizen Club on crime prevention. He decided to focus on Saturday trips a member can take with a ghetto kid to historical sites, Little League events, and museums. The trips could be a get-acquainted time. The PR man chose the working title, "Saturday Trips That Can Help Check Crime."

*Talkamatics tip #105: A working title serves to keep your speech planning on target.* Later, on, in Chapter 9, I'll show you how you can pare and polish your working title.

## Easy-Do Outlining

After you get your working title, you'll need to develop a target-reaching main-point outline. You can make a simple outline by putting down three or four main points you want to bring out. ***Talkamatics tip #106: State these main points in complete sentences.*** For Williams' speech an outline might run:

1. The mobile executive faces these home buying/selling problems.

2. Real estate firms throughout the U.S. have developed a money-saving purchase plan.

3. Here are specific instances where the plan has worked successfully.

4. How you can learn more about this plan.

## Rapid Researching

Once you get your main-point outline, stop and think coolly before you gather information. Many speeches earn low marks because speakers make one of two mistakes in information-gathering:

a) The most common mistake is that the speaker doesn't use *enough interesting, specific illustrations.*

b) The second mistake is that he does *too much undirected research.*

Recalling that people say, "Research, research, research your speech," the over-zealous speaker-to-be begins to look madly through files, magazines and books at home, his office and the library.

He hasn't main-point-outlined his speech so he doesn't know what he's looking for. The result? He gets research-pooped-out. His research turns up a great deal of vague information, which he crams into a too-long speech. What happens? The audience rates him as a speaker who's dull, dreary, depressing!

Yet this research fiasco doesn't have to happen if you remember ***Talkamatics tip #107: As you research, look for information to persuasively illustrate the main points.*** Don't roam all over the lot looking for every stray bit of information.

In researching on-target illustrations for your main points, use two sources:

- People
- Print

Often the best "people" source is your own knowledge about your work or hobby. Mike Williams, speaking about the real estate plan, might talk to salesmen who've sold, and buyers who've bought, homes under the plan.

The office manager talking about leasing plants might get comments from the receptionist about visitors' remarks and comments from the representative of the company from which she leased the plants.

A speaker talking of Saturday trips with ghetto kids could talk to the kids as well as to adults who've made similar trips, and get comments from them.

So talk to people and get compelling firsthand information.

For print sources, keep your main points in mind and then go into your files, books and magazines on your shelves, as well as material from your trade association. Next, check with the librarian at your local library for research help. When you research, here's *Talkamatics tip #108: Stay on the alert for Talkamatics dazzlers.*

## Talkamatics Dazzlers

One witty speaker likes to ask himself, "What are little speeches made of?" Then he'll answer, "Statistics, quotes and anecdotes."

So when you research your main points, assemble a mix of illustrations. These illustrations, anecdotes, stories, statistics, quotes, statements of authority, comparisons and analogies, are what we call Talkamatics dazzlers. They can turn a good speech into a great one.

As you research, when you come across a Talkamatics dazzler, copy it on a 3″x 5″ index card. Be sure to note on the card its source. For instance, if it's from a book, give the title, author's name, publisher, publication date and page number. Then copy the dazzler. Be sure to copy your information exactly. On quoted remarks, use quotation marks and the source. In the right-hand corner of each card use the appropriate Talkamatics symbol. These symbols are:

Anecdote or story—0
Statistic—//
Statement of authority—=
Comparison or analogy—U

As you research, keep shuffling through your research cards to see that you have a variety of persuasive illustrations. By studying the symbols in the right-hand corner you can more readily see if you're collecting a good mix of illustrations than by merely looking at a group of words on the index cards.

If you find you're topheavy on statistics and quotes, drop your research along those lines and look for anecdotes and stories.

Collect your illustrations as quickly as possible. Once you've settled on what you'll talk about, you'll run into good illustrations on every hand—from your own experience, TV programs, newspapers and magazines you glance at. **Talkamatics tip #109:** *There seems to be a law of attraction that often brings the dazzlers you need in your speechmaking to your attention easily.*

## The Grabber-Lasso-What-Socko-Pattern

When you draft your speech, you want it to have four distinct parts:

1. A strong opening that in effect *grabs* your audience's interest.

2. A sentence or two that tells why the subject is important to the audience. These sentences *lasso* your audience's interest and keep 'em listening.

3. The body. The persuasive *main points* you want to bring out, illustrated with Talkamatics dazzlers.

4. A conclusion that's *socko*.

Now if you observe the above closely, you'll get that old familiar feeling. Why? Because it's merely an *expansion* of your 1-2-3 Magic Package module. For example, points one and two provide your statement of purpose; point three, the specifics; and point four, a restatement of purpose and sometimes a call for action.

Since by now you've probably had good results with the talk modules given earlier, I'm sure you'll feel confident that you can do the same thing with this "big speech" module. And you'll be right because it's a terrific success module!

So let's look closely at the beginning or grabber in the speaker's success module.

## The Talkamatics Grabber

Your grabber opening needs to be crisp, fascinating, with a lot of sit-up-and-listen appeal to your audience. So think over your research, and remember you want to *grab* your audience! Do you have a strong statement, or a problem to open with? Using the real estate subject cited earlier, Williams might kick off with:

(*Statement.*) "Today I'm going to tell you about a new real estate purchase plan when you buy a new home that could save you from $2000 to $10,000."

(*Problem.*) "Did you ever move to a town, couldn't find the right home, and shelled out several thousand dollars in rent before you found a place that met your requirements?"

Besides a strong statement or problem, you could form a grabber opening with statistics, anecdotes, a quotation, a comparison, or a combination of these. So look through your Talkamatics dazzlers and shape up a compelling opening rather than drably saying, "Today I would like to tell you of our new trial purchase plan for homes." Next, prepare the Talkamatics lasso.

## The Talkamatics Lasso

After you've grabbed your listeners' attention, you must prevent them from wandering down thinking byways— worrying about a memo they need to dictate, a phone call they should make, or planning a tennis game with a crony. You can lasso their interest and tighten the lasso so firmly they can't mentally escape. You can do this by telling them why the subject is important to *them*. For the two opening illustrations given earlier, the "you" lasso might be:

1. "You executives are mobile. You're here today and tomorrow you may be transferred. This plan can help you."

2. "That needn't happen again. Because now there's a new try-out home-buying plan that can save you several thousands of dollars."

Usually your lasso takes only a few sentences. Then add a couple of sentences to give a roadmap of where you're going. Often the roadmap is a summary of what you'll talk about. In the real estate example, your roadmap might be:

"In my talk today, I'll touch on some problems of buying real estate the conventional way, how a new plan has been worked out throughout the country, and how you, or a co-worker, can take advantage of the plan. To begin with...."

## The Talkamatics "What"

In your research, you collected a good mix of Talkamatics dazzlers—including anecdotes, quotations, statistics—to illustrate your main points. To line up what you'll talk about in the body of your speech, take your main points and put appropriate subpoints under them. For instance, in the real estate speech the pattern might look like this:

1. The mobile executive faces these home buying/selling problems:

    a) Transferred
    b) Loss of money
    c) Home unsatisfactory

Now note, in both words and the Talkamatics dazzler symbols, the illustrations you'll use to put across your subpoints. Doing this, the above outline would become:

    1. The mobile executive faces these home buying/selling problems:
    a) Transferred.
       Difficulty in selling (2 anecdotes) (00)
    b) Loss of money.
       The Powell survey (statistic) (//)
    c) New home unsatisfactory.
       Remarks about previous home (comparison) (U)

To make a final check that you have varied illustrations, re-do your outline in picture language—with a long line for each main point, a broken line for each subpoint, and Talkamatics dazzler symbols for the illustrations. The picture language outline of the above will look like this:

1._____

    a)_ _ _ _ _ _ _ _ _ _ _ _ _ _ _ _

      0 0

    b)_ _ _ _ _ _ _ _ _ _ _ _ _ _ _ _

      //

    c)_ _ _ _ _ _ _ _ _ _ _ _ _ _ _

      U

By outlining your speech like this you can more readily see if your appropriate material contains varied Talkamatics dazzlers than if you use merely a word outline.

*Talkamatics tip #110: Should you use, say, too many slanted lines (statistics) or too many horseshoes (comparisons), your speech will seem topheavy in statistics or comparisons.*

*Talkamatics tip #111: If you skip all statistics, your speech will seem flabby, not concrete.*

*Talkamatics tip #112: If you omit anecdotes, your speech will lack sparkle.*

## Ending with a Talkamatics Socko

Have you ever noticed how you enjoy a neat ending—an anecdote or a striking quotation—on a magazine article?

Isn't it great to get a letter with a friendly, unusual closing, something with a little zip to it?

And ever observed how pleased you are when a TV or radio announcer puts a fillip into his sign-off?

You want to please your audience with a Talkamatics socko ending. Generally, there are two types of socko endings:

**1. A strong recap of your grabber.** Example: "It will definitely pay you to look into this new home-purchase plan that can save you from $2000 to $10,000."

**2. The upbeat action ending.** In this type of ending you tell the audience what you want them to do. If possible, you add an incentive for them to do this. In the real estate speech, Williams might say, "Now in conclusion, I'm going to pass out a kit that gives you all the details of the new home purchase plan...plus a $200 bonus coupon. If you or a friend you recommend purchase a home under this new plan within the next year, you'll receive a $200 bonus."

Either of these endings will let you conclude with plenty of socko.

Following these easy Talkamatics steps will help you lay the foundation for a knockout talk. But resultful rehearsing (see next chapter) can turn your speech from gauche to good—and even very, very good! And remember, a first-rate talk can help bring you prestige, pay hikes and promotions.

## Chapter Check-Back

• *Shaping a subject.* If you're asked to speak on a subject which poses a problem for you, don't hesitate to shape it, mold it, so you can handle it easily. Get an okay from the program chairman on this subject revision.

• *Filling in an audience size-up sheet* will greatly help you prepare a failure-free speech that will fascinate your audience.

• *Having a working title* will insure keeping your speech in focus as you develop it.

• *Developing three or four main points,* expressed in complete sentences, will give you your basic outline.

• *Beginning* with a grabber opening will rivet your audience's attention. You can find a grabber in your collection of Talkamatics dazzlers.

• *Lassoing interest* with a couple of sentences about why your subject is important to your audience will keep your listeners' attention from straying.

• *Illustrating your main points* with some sparkling Talkamatics dazzler illustrations such as anecdotes, stories, statistics, comparisons, analogies, statements of authorities, will keep your audience absorbed in your talk.

• *Selecting a good ending* from your research lets you conclude with socko.

• *Utilizing the "speed" factor.* As soon as you accept a speech invitation, work fast, fast, fast to draft your speech. By saving maximum time for rehearsing (see next chapter), the more striking a speech you'll give.

# Nine

# Rehearsing for Results
# with Talkamatics

A journalist once lay in a hammock on his patio where his five-year-old daughter was playing. She asked him to tell her a story. "Well," he hedged, "wait a minute till a story comes to me."

After a minute or two, she impatiently nudged him in the ribs and said, "Stories don't come to you. You go to them."

It's the same with finding rehearsal time. It never comes to you. When you plan to give a talk, your activities, by some pesky law, accelerate. You have less time than ever.

With these problems, should you rehearse? And if so, how do you work in rehearsals?

The answer to the first question is you should rehearse, rehearse, even if you make only a short talk on departmental procedures. Rehearsals separate the men from the boys in talking well. And a well-done talk starts turning just-a-job into an UP-TRENDING CAREER.

As for question number two, the Talkamatics system calls for the "I'm-going-underground" approach to rehearsing.

This means going *underground* for a few weeks. You'll need to skip a few church, civic, club meetings, household chores, TV-watching or someone's birthday celebration. You must get ruthless. Cut out some activities.

Now, it's harder to do, but you must mentally go underground at work, too. How? Don't volunteer for those extra jobs that make it necessary to take home your briefcase. Put off an out-of-town trip.

   ***Talkamatics tip #113:*** *Give your best energies to your rehearsals.*

   Later, you can quickly make up for your undergrounding. And believe me, the results of delivering a super talk, the kind that causes your career to climb, will justify your means.

   How many rehearsals do you need? A Talkamatics rule of thumb is to allot at least one-third of the time you use to prepare a talk to practicing it.

   To illustrate: If you accept an invitation to speak three weeks from today, plan on two weeks to prepare the speech and one week for rehearsing.

   However, if you want your speech to *really* zing across, ***Talkamatics tip #114*** is to *spend two-thirds of your preparation time in rehearsing.*

## Five Secrets of Rehearsal Time

   Here are five secrets of using your rehearsal time effectively:

   **1. Spot several rehearsal times throughout the day for a number of days.** By stretching out your rehearsals you'll gain far more from your rehearsal time.

   **2. Practice during off-beat times.** Close your office door, or borrow someone's office or the company conference room and rehearse during your lunch hour. I know a supervisor in a suburban factory who takes a noon stroll through the countryside, running through his speech as he walks.

   **3. Try a bathroom rehearsal.** In the small area of the bathroom, cup your hand to your ear and listen. Does your speech sound well, your enunciation distinct, your voice firm and vigorous? If your enunciation seems sloppy or your voice faltering, give special attention to these problems and correct them—that is, enunciate with clarity or deliver your words with more vigor.

**4. As soon as you're familiar with your speech, start practicing before a full-length mirror.** Use gesturing and any props, including visual aids, you'll need. If your props aren't available, use substitutes. A lamp, placed on a table in front of you, can act as your microphone. If a chart isn't ready, put a sheet of cardboard on a chair beside you. When your speech calls for pointing to the chart, or flipping a page, do so.

*Talkamatics tip #115: Never omit use of a prop (or its stand-in) during rehearsals.*

**5. Call a dress rehearsal.** Gather together a few people—perhaps the ones you work with—during a lunch hour and give your talk. Explain to them the type of audience you'll talk to and ask them to consider this when making comments.

Their reactions will show parts you may wish to change or leave out. John Lawson, media researcher for a Chicago advertising agency, did this. The polishing enabled him to give a remarkably good talk; compliments about his speaking know-how were heard throughout the agency. The presentation marked him a "comer," and the agency gave him more opportunities to speak, then promotions, then the title of vice president.

## Planning Your Visual Aids

How soon do you plan and implement your visual aids? Ideally, the day you say, "Yes, I'll talk to your group." However, you often must wait a few days till you decide on the focus of your remarks and do enough research to know what visual aids you'll need.

In Chapter 5 you found ideas for successfully employing visuals. You may wish to brush up on these procedures.

When you plan your visuals, don't forget **Talkamatics tip #116:** *Make all visual aids large enough so the audience can see them clearly.*

## Guideline for Humor

As you rehearse, you may decide you'll add some humor to your talk. Here are five target-reaching ways to do so:

*Target-reacher #1:* Your *opening* remarks are a choice place to use an amusing anecdote or joke.

*Target-reacher #2:* Don't use *unrelated* humor. Tell a funny story to emphasize a point you make. For example, you might use a joke about someone's over-spending to illustrate the need for careful business budgeting.

*Target-reacher #3:* Instead of long, involved jokes try to use one-liners or short jokes. Example: "When a customer, waiting to turn his car over for servicing, complained to the auto service manager, he replied, 'What do you mean slow service? We haven't given you any yet!' " Short jokes don't tire an audience and you don't run as much danger of fluffing.

*Target-reacher #4:* How do you find funny stories? One way—remodel jokes to fit your talk. To illustrate: When preparing a talk about mistakes I'd made on my first job, I read a joke about a man who'd come to his first job in a food factory fired with enthusiasm. He proved so inept, he felt he would soon be fired the same way. I adapted the joke to my situation and earned chuckles.

*Target-reacher #5:* Beware of humor others may know. In other words, don't use a last month's *Reader's Digest* joke in your remarks to a civic group...or a currently "making the rounds" industry joke for a company talk. But how do you pull fresh stories out of the air?

**Talkamatics tip #117:** *When searching for fresh funnies, use the humorous things that happen to you, your friends, relatives and business associates.*

## Memorizing Your Opening

After the first couple of rehearsals, try this automatic: Memorize the words of your opening. For example, in the speech mentioned in the last chapter, the opening might run:

"Today I'm going to tell you about a new real estate plan when you buy a home that could save you from $2000 to $10,000."

If this were your opening, you'd memorize the words and use them every time you rehearse. Don't deviate from them. This is accident-stutter-goof-up insurance. Because even if your introducer surprises you by presenting you as the president of your company and you're in the lower echelon, after you make a little comment on the goof, you'll go smoothly into your opening.

What happens if you *don't* memorize your opening? As you start out, you'll grope for words. And when you grope you often fluff. A mini case history:

Allen Redman of Baltimore, a business friend of mine, once directed a half-hour TV show on an educational channel. He felt fortunate because one of the participants was a professional actress. From their first rehearsal, she knew her words perfectly. But in the last studio rehearsal, minutes before going on the air, she confessed she didn't feel comfortable in her opening line. Could she, she asked, recast it slightly?

Over-ruling an inner voice that said "No," my friend Allen let her tinker with a few words. Sure enough, as they went on the air, she fluffed her opening line. And the show got off to a weak start.

## Achieving the Right-on-the-Button Closing

At the same time you set your opening in concrete, another time-saver automatic is to memorize your closing. And rehearse it in those *exact* words.

Usually, you chisel out a strong closing that depends on a certain word sequence. In the example speech in the last word chapter, the ending might shape up: "In closing, I repeat, it definitely will pay you to look into this new home purchase plan. It can save you from $2000 to $10,000."

If this were your ending, you'd memorize each of these words in this precise order. Should you grope for words, the statement may not sound nearly so effective. In fact you may goof, and thus end without professional flair.

Right now, I'm carving out a closing for a talk where I plan to ask club members for support for a project of sharing books with the community.

Since I felt lazy, I decided not to memorize my closing, but to wing it. During my first rehearsal I found myself saying:

"And so our committee would like to ask for your help— er, your support—in this share-a-book project—er—in the community."

I knew I sounded awful so...another try. It came out:

"And now a word about our important sharing project; I'd like to ask your support."

These miserable closings unlazied me and I got down to memorizing this strong closing:

"And in closing, the committee asks for your support in this important share-a-book project!"

**Talkamatics tip #118** is *develop a right-on-the-button closing, memorize it, and rehearse using the same words.*

Although you memorize your opening and closing, never memorize the body of your speech.

If you've ever lived near a bakery, darted out and bought bread or pastries fresh from the oven, taken them home and eaten them immediately, you know how good things are when they're fresh.

This is true when you speak. Nothing sounds so great to listeners as fresh, unmemorized words. The words you spontaneously choose are usually very *right* words.

Another point in favor of fresh, spontaneous delivery is that you probably won't speak too fast, because you have to think what you'll say next. Audiences like to see a speaker's face as he thinks, and perhaps mentally searches for a word. Thinking as you talk makes your face, inflection, delivery sound professional. You won't sound like a school kid saying a memorized piece.

So every time you practice, use your memorized opening and closing, then line up your main points and illustrations, become familiar with them, but voice them in fresh words.

A bonus point to this technique is it makes rehearsals more interesting, too. You almost unconsciously find yourself honing your material, your choice of words, what you brief, what you expand, so your speech becomes potent and persuasive.

## Assembling Your Key-Word Outline

As you familiarize yourself with the body (module) of your speech, jot down a capsule outline. This will look like a grocery list with about eight to 12 key words to remind you of essential points. Plan to take your key-word outline with you, and consult it, if need be, during your speech.

## Five Steps to Psyching Out Fear

About now, in your rehearsal time, you begin to feel fear nips: "What if I'm really nervous giving my talk? What if I shake? What if I forget part of my talk? What if these nutty nervous nudgings inside me cause me to give a poor talk? Is there anything I can do *now to curtail the fear I may feel?*"

Yes. Use these five steps to psyching out fear:

**1. The take-off step.** About a week before your talk, sit down and, in vivid detail, picture yourself arriving to deliver your remarks. Start with your take-off from your office, say, to make a talk in the company conference room.

Picture *specifically* your departure, including such things as what you'll wear, how you'll transport your props, at what point you'll put your key-word outline in your pocket, what time you'll leave.

As these situations flash before your eyes, consider roadblocks that might come up and how you'll handle them. For instance, if you get a delaying phone call, will you take it or not? What if someone buttonholes you on the way to the conference room? How will you handle the buttonholer?

**2. The arrival step.** Next, visualize what will happen when you arrive. If it's in your company conference room, will you want to set up your props before the others get there? Will you want to write something ahead of time on the blackboard? Will you personally want to make sure everyone has a pad and paper?

If you'll talk outside your company—say at a club meeting room—and are not able to visit the place ahead of time, will you encounter problems finding it? In the event of a problem, do you have a name and phone number to call for someone to "guide" you to the spot?

When you arrive at your location, what will you do? Carry in your props? Or first check with the chairman, then bring in your props? Then how will you proceed? Visualize everything you can about your arrival.

**3. The interim step.** Next, visualize how you'll handle the interim, from your arrival until you speak. If mingling with the guests, will you pace yourself, not try to be extra jolly in the jolly time? Instead, will you take it easy, get in with a group where there's a good holder-forth and let him hold forth, so you'll stay untired and fresh?

There's nothing like a sparkling drink or two to take the sparkle out of a speaker. So *Talkamatics tip #119* is *visualize the cocktail hour and see yourself sipping only a soft drink.*

As you consider, in your mind's eye, the conference or club meeting room where you'll be, envision who else will be there. What problems might arise? If there are several speakers, and they run too long, what can you cut out of *your* talk to even up the time?

**4. The TIGA step.** The tuning-in-gratitude-and-appreciation step is important. See yourself waiting to deliver your speech or presentation and feeling grateful. "About what?" you ask. About any number of things. In the Talkamatics system, we start with the obvious.

For example, a Talkamatics speaker might think while he's waiting, "I'm grateful this group asked me to give a talk; I'm grateful I did a *solid* job of preparing my talk; I'm grateful I have something helpful (or interesting) to say; I'm grateful these people came to hear me talk." He can, of course, expand on this line of thinking.

But do you see the point in this fear-combating step? It's to flood your thinking with grateful, appreciative thoughts. See yourself, during the interim step, as not worrying about how you'll do, whether your voice will sound okay, and so on.

Picture yourself sitting there *appreciating* what you'll talk about and your audience. Appreciation dynamites fear because it takes thought off yourself.

**Talkamatics tip #120** is grateful, appreciative thinking is a terrific mental sauna bath. It'll help you relax, and then you can appear at your best.

I recall talking occasions when I've been scared blue. But as I began pouring out grateful thinking, the tension flowed out and I was able to make good—and sometimes great-sounding—remarks.

Grateful thinking also helped Irving Francis of Bridgeport, Connecticut, lift his speaking ability many notches. Irving, who has his own plumbing/heating/air conditioning firm, always feared sales presentations and talks before local clubs.

But he told me one night he tried the Talkamatics target-reaching method of feeling gratitude and appreciation as he sat waiting to speak. The result? He made a speech

different from any he'd **ever** delivered. He was free of fear,
and in his own words,"...made *tremendous contact* with my
audience. For the first time, I had a talk go over BIG!"

**5. The enthusiasm step.** As you go about psyching out
fear with the above steps, also try this fear-eraser: Start
rehearsing with *enthusiasm.*

But how do you become zestful when you practice? To
project enthusiasm, you must *act* as if you were:

a) Talking to your most favorite friends—people you'd
rather talk to than any others you know; and

b) Telling them the most informative, concrete,
fascinating things about a new company procedure or your
department's reorganization or the most absorbing,
surprising, useful things possible about grandfather-clock-
making or whatever.

Appropriate action follows thought. And when your
thought is ebullient, you'll speak enthusiastically—and thus
self-confidently.

When Fran Blair of Houston, Texas was widowed, she
had three kids and a mother to support. She took a job as a
supermarket checker. Her lack of education prevented her
from getting a better job. She did, however, enroll in a public
speaking course.

When she was assigned her first talk, she said, "I felt
fearful—like an icicle. It seemed hard to follow my
instructor's advice: to speak *enthusiastically.*"

But she tried. Grateful that she could take the course,
she mustered all the zest she could.

The result? That night she won a small prize for the best,
most enthusiastic talk. And she went on to win other
speaking prizes, a new job as a sales person, bonuses, sales
prizes of trips to glamorous foreign spots and an excellent
annual income.

So remember **Talkamatics tip #121:** *When you rehearse
with enthusiasm, you melt fear.*

## Foolproof Timing of Your Speech

After the first week of rehearsals, record your speech on a tape recorder, and get an exact timing. *Talkamatics tip #122: Generally don't let a daytime speech run over 20 minutes, and an after-dinner speech 15 minutes.*

Notice, in timing your speech, it's not enough to merely clock it. Why? Because during rehearsals you often start to smooth over a portion or repeat something with greater emphasis. Then you incorrectly estimate how much time out you took. So *Talkamatics tip #123* is *use a tape recorder in timing your speech.*

If you're ten or 15 minutes over time, the pro way is to drop a whole main point. But if you're just four or five minutes over, drop an illustration or two.

Be precise about cutting to the proper time, or even a little under it. Again, because of television, and seeing professional entertainment, audiences don't like to hear speakers run a minute over their time allowances.

## Eye-Locking Rehearsals

By the second week of your rehearsals, make sure you research with eye contact. Picture the mirror you rehearse before as your imaginary audience.

From now on, as you rehearse, practice locking eyes with various members of the audience in different parts of the room.

This technique often is called "eye-sweeping," but it calls for actual eye contact, not a vague, unfocused or "sweeping over" look, at various parts of the room. Be sure you look into the eyes of a number of people, in different areas, long enough to make contact with them. Talk to one person for several seconds, then move your gaze to another.

So important is eye-locking that even if you forget entirely a part of your speech, but keep good eye contact, your audience will rate you as an extremely good speaker.

**Talkamatics tip #124:** *Don't wait till you deliver your speech; practice eye contact during your rehearsals.*

And if you want to put extra shekels in your pocket in the future, heed **Talkamatics tip #125:** *In a spontaneous talk, employ eye-locking 100% of the time.*

## Adding Plenty of Body Language

Now, with your rehearsals underway, let me remind you to beef up your body language, not only in quantity but also in quality. Make sure your rehearsal gestures are fairly large, apt and varied.

If need be, review some of the body language goodies in Chapter 7. Remember, you'll automatically drop a number of gestures when you actually give your talk. So rehearse with a generous amount of non-verbal language.

## Sizzling Your Title

In Chapter 8, you learned how to give your talk a working title to keep your subject in focus.

Now brief and sizzle your title.

For example, real estate manager Mike Williams might shorten his working title of "A Money-Saving Home-Buying Plan for Mobile Executives" to "A Money-Saving Home-Buying Plan" or "Try-Buy Home Purchase Plan."

The office manager who selected the working title, "How You Can Decorate Thriftily by Leasing Plants," might sharpen her title to "Lease a Leaf" or "Penny-Pinching Plant Decorating."

And the PR man, suggesting possible outings for ghetto kids to club members, might telescope his title of "Saturday Trips That Can Help Check Crime" to "Fight Crime with Fun" or "Funday Crime Fighting."

Here are two guides for polishing your title: (1) Keep it short—preferably six words or less; and (2) try to include a listener-benefit, a play on words, humor or intrigue, or a combination of these.

The more appealing and/or loaded with listener-benefits your title, the more favorable effect it'll have on your listeners.

Mike Williams decided to hone his title to "A Money-Saving Home-Buying Plan."

## Your Speech Prop Cache

At the same time as you start rehearsing (or even as early as you start planning your speech), collect your speech props, including visual aids, in one spot.

Be careful what spot you use. Make sure it's a secure place, preferably one you can lock. I recall one consulting firm executive, Fred Pendleton of Oklahoma City, who was slated to give a speech. He began to collect his props in a 24" x 28" portfolio that belonged to the firm. The day of his speech he went to get the portfolio and couldn't find it. Anywhere.

He was ready to go without his props—and in his case, without them his speech would fail—when another exec breezed in. He'd taken the portfolio the night before, emptied the props into his car trunk, used the portfolio to collect materials from a client, and now was returning it and the props.

So **Talkamatics tip #126** is *put your visual aids in a safe place, where nobody can get them.*

And **Talkamatics tip #127** is *if you have a number of smaller props, a suitcase works well. If you use a large flip chart, you can carry it under your arm.*

## When Should You Read Your Speech?

Talkamatics teaches to talk extemporaneously whenever possible. However, you may need to read your talk when:

1) You lack time to rehearse properly so you can give a smooth talk;

2) The factual or technical nature of the subject makes it difficult to give your talk without reading;

3) You may be speaking for your company and don't want to mis-speak or be misunderstood.

## Preparing Talk/Read Cards

If you decide to write and read your talk, Talkamatics advises, "Don't torture your listeners by reading a dull manuscript talk." Instead use this helpful hint—talk/read cards. Here's how to make these little life preservers:

1. *Write your talk as briefly as possible.* Use simple words. Don't use complicated sentences or their complexity probably will cause you either to stumble or to sound monotonous.

2. *Type your talk triple-spaced on 5" x 8" index cards.* Leave wide margins. Number the cards in sequence. I prefer typing a talk on cards rather than on 8½" x 11" white paper. Why? Because you constantly set aside a card as you read. This movement helps keep your voice vibrant. Also you tend to glance at the audience more often. You don't run as much risk of burying your head in a manuscript page, and slowly inching your way down a page in boring, boring, boring caterpillar style. Another thing: When you use talk/read cards, you write briefer, punchier, *talkier* talks—the kind listeners yearn for!

3. *A sample card.* Exactly how does a talk/read card look? Here's how one, prepared by Mike Williams for his new home buying/selling plan talk mentioned in Chapter 8, might look:

> *Card #1*
> "Did you ever move to a town...couldn't find the right home...and shelled out several thousand dollars in rent...before you found a place that met your requirements? Today's mobile executive faces this—and other—home buying/selling problems in this city...."

When he gets to an anecdote, Mike will look up and tell it from memory.

*Talkamatics tip #128:* Told from memory, in fresh words on the spot, the anecdote sounds far more vital than if read.

4. *Marking your talk/read cards.* In order to talk more vividly, mark the various words and passages you wish to emphasize on your cards with felt-tip pens in various colors. The different colors will make the directions pop out. Note any directions like "slow down" or "pause" in margin. Use an arrow pointing up to remind you to raise your voice, an arrow pointing down to lower it.

To remember to "color" a word—that is, if the word is "smooth" and you want to emphasize it by pronouncing it as "smo-o-oth" or if the word is "exciting" and you want to pronounce it so it sounds truly "exciting!"—circle it. Perhaps you want to stress other words by increasing the volume of your voice; underline these words. Indicate a pause between phrases with a slash.

## Rehearsing a Written Talk

1. *Be so familiar with what you'll read,* you can merely glance at your talk, take in several sentences at a gulp, and "say" them looking directly at your listeners. Talkamatics calls this the "flick-glance" technique. You should use eye-technique 85% of the time.

*Talkamatics tip #129:* The flick-glance technique can turn an average speech reader into an ace.

2. *Read a talk as if you're speaking, not reading.* Use zestful delivery.

3. *Employ body language.*

4. *Every so often, if appropriate, smile at your audience.*

5. *Rehearse sufficiently*—generally from eight to 20 times.

And here's an encouraging thought. *Talkamatics tip #130:* Even though you must rehearse carefully, a talk/read speech won't need as much get-ready time as extemporaneous speaking.

## A Manager's Talk/Reading Success

Stephanie Chang, community relations manager of a glass-making factory in North Carolina, recently accepted an invitation to talk to a local civic group.

With only ten days to prepare her speech, and because she would be using many figures and statistics and wanted to give them correctly, Stephanie decided to talk/read her speech from 5″ x 8″ cards as described above.

Stephanie told me she rehearsed talk/reading the speech 18 times—three times a day, for six days— before she gave it.

The result? Stephanie skillfully flick-read her talk. Most people thought she talked off the cuff. "Oh, I noticed she hauled out notes," said one listener, "but thank heaven she didn't use them. I hate to listen to people who read speeches. Hers was a powerful talk!"

So here's **Talkamatics tip #131:** *If you don't wish to use off-the-cuff delivery, use the talk/read card method outlined above...and you'll begin to see fabulous improvement when you read your remarks.*

## Handling Your Talk Publicity

Some time during your rehearsal period, a business associate or meeting chairman may ask you for background information to use in introducing you as a speaker.

Many people, with an up-to-date resume, simply forward a photo copy. Or you may wish to type out a simple background sheet, giving the title of your talk and a few pertinent facts, such as your name, business title, name of your business firm, job responsibilities and any other info that helps establish you as a pro on the subject you'll talk on.

Yet, though you may rehearse, for complete success in talking you'll want to know Talkamatics techniques for putting over the big speech. You'll learn these in the next chapter.

## Chapter Check-Back

• *Planning*. For a speech three weeks distant, Talkamatics suggests two weeks get-ready time, one week rehearsal. Even better, one week preparation, two weeks rehearsal.

• *Scheduling rehearsals*. Rehearse at several *different* times during your day, over a period of days. Recommended: bathroom rehearsals to check your enunciation; mirror rehearsals including use of visual aids (or stand-ins); and pre-testing your talk on friends who'll comment on any weaknesses.

• *Planning and executing your visual aids* should start early in the rehearsal period.

• *Spicing your talk with humor* means using one-liners instead of lengthy jokes when possible. Also employ *related* humor—jokes that emphasize a point you make. To present fresh funnies, draw on amusing things that happen to you, your family, relatives, business associates.

• *Preparing a key-word outline* can provide security. This outline should look like a grocery list with about eight to 12 words to remind you of main and subpoints.

• *Psyching out fear* can be done by visualizing what is coming up, feeling grateful for your speaking opportunity, and rehearsing with enthusiasm.

• *Fool-proof timing of speech*. Tape record it during rehearsal, then cut, if necessary. Generally, the maximum time for a day speech is 20 minutes, for an after-dinner talk, 15 minutes.

• *Employing body language and 100% eye-contact* are musts in rehearsing a spontaneous talk.

• *Utilizing a safe storage spot* for your props and visual aids will prevent slip-ups.

• *Writing a speech?* Talkamatics advises using 5″ x 8″ cards with your talk written in simple words, short sentences, and typed triple space.

• *Rehearsing a written talk* is done by reading it as if you were conversing with your listeners...taking in several sentences at a glance...using body language...maintaining eye-contact 85% of the time...and employing enthusiasm. To read  a talk smoothly, you should rehearse eight to 20 times.

# Ten

# The Talkamatics Method of Putting Over the Big Speech

When Mike Williams, anticipating his upcoming speech, steps into the Distribution Club meeting room, his mental attitude will greatly influence the success of his speech. If he can maintain a right mental outlook, he'll stay fresh, buoyant, and able to turn out an outstanding speech.

But how can he achieve and keep this good mental attitude? The best recipe I know is to *love your listeners.*

## RX for Loving Thy Listeners

In the previous chapter, you read about feeling gratitude and appreciation during your rehearsals for your future audience. This is Loving Thy Listeners. Now, when the big day of your talk arrives, you must *continue* to love thy listeners.

Why? Because this Talkamatics technique is a success tool. Loving Thy Listeners helps keep your thought off yourself, helps keep you from suffering the talking shakes and quakes most people feel, and even helps to keep you from forgetting parts of your presentation.

So, *Talkamatics tip #132: On the day of your talk, vigorously love thy listeners by feeling gratitude and appreciation for them.*

Accountant Herb Selig of Sacramento, California, found LTL a life preserver in talking. In fact, he told me that the first time he became free of fear and tension in speaking was when he applied this Talkamatics target-reaching method.

Here's part of the letter Herb wrote about what happened when he addressed the local chapter of a national accounting society:

"When I arrived, I found my thoughts were constantly zeroing inward on myself. 'What would the group think of me? Could I remember my opening? What if I forgot some of my main points? My voice feels weak,' and so on.

"Well, I started to change this worried thought pattern. When a thought like, 'What will they think of me?' popped up, I'd say to myself, 'The important thing is what do I think of them?' And looking around, I'd think, gratefully, 'Looks like they did a good job of inviting the members...getting the tables set up....'

"Continuing to think *outward*, I was able to give a waitress a hand with moving a table...help the meeting chairman locate a member....

"I enjoyed talking to the people during dinner. And when I stood up to speak, I had a warm feeling for that group, and felt relaxed and confident. People laughed at my jokes, listened to my points, and were interesting in their questions. In closing the meeting the chairman commented, 'You made one of the best talks we've ever had!' "

So, **Talkamatics tip #133:** *When you arrive to give a talk, focus your thoughts outward appreciatively on others.*

You may not be able to do as many tangible things as Herb Selig did but you can think constructively about your listeners. This LTL thinking will show up in a more-at-ease you and a better talk.

Now, the upcoming tips will also aid you in putting across a winning presentation. Begin with this safety parachute...

## Suggested: A Scouting Mission

In the last chapter, you learned during your rehearsal period to "imagine" in detail your arrival to speak.

Now, if possible, go further and advance-scout the actual location a day or two in advance. A story that goes the rounds in Southern business circles points up what happens when you don't advance-scout.

One day, in Memphis, Tennessee, a Georgia tennis coach blew into town to discuss his coaching philosophy with 60 high school coaches at a Southeastern prep school clinic. He rushed right to the Holiday Inn, into a private dining room, sat down and began talking with some of the men about tennis.

"A couple of the guys seemed real interested," recalled the coach, "so finally I asked one where he coached and he said he was a hospital X-ray technician, attending this technicians' conference.

"That was when I discovered," said the coach, "there was more than one Holiday Inn in the city and I was in the wrong one."

While that's an extreme example, often a business person is notified a week before a meeting where it'll be held. He arrives at the company Conference Room A to give his talk—and finds there's another meeting going on. He then hunts up his new location and perhaps ends up late for the meeting...and discovers in his new location, there's no blackboard, or corkboard walls to pin exhibits on, and he'd planned to do just that.

**Talkamatics tip #134: Check out your room a day or so before your talk.**

Size up the equipment. Will there be everything you'll need: a table on which to put a slide projector, easel, etc.; and needs for the group—ash trays, note pads, carafe of water, glasses, whatever?

Study the set-up of chairs. If you'll talk to a small group, here's a suggestion: Arrange the chairs in a semicircle, join the group and make your talk informally rather than have people sit on chairs in classroom style with you up front expounding.

If you talk to four people at a conference table for 12, ask them to sit together at one end. (Sometimes for a club talk, you'll find chairs set up for, say, 80 members and only 30 arrive. When that happens, ask that the extra chairs be removed or roped off. In other words, don't let 30 people spread out over 80 chairs.)

*Talkamatics tip #135: By grouping your listeners in one part of the room, you can direct your remarks to one area—and make a punchier talk.*

During your scouting session, talk with the conference room scheduler. Request that you be personally notified *as soon as possible* if there's a room change. Sometimes a half hour's notice can make the difference in your rounding up things you'll need for a location that's been changed—and utlimately will determine the success of your talk.

If you can't scout in advance, at least get to your talk premises from one-half to an hour ahead of time and review the set-up.

*Talkamatics tip #136: Never rely entirely on others for arrangements where you'll make a talk. Advance check on them yourself.*

## What to Wear

In putting over a persuasive talk, what you wear plays an important part. It's advisable to consult the program chairman on how to dress.

My thought is one dresses in character for his role in the business world, in keeping with his speech subject and the specific type and time of the meeting. To illustrate:

• If a photographer talks on his work at a mid-morning meeting, it seems appropriate for him to dress in a "good" version of his work clothes—that is, a turtleneck sweater, suede jacket, checked pants, and boots would look fine.

• On the other hand, if a banker speaks about prime interest rates to a lunch meeting of businessmen, it would be fitting for him to wear a business suit and color coordinated shirt and tie.

When a woman speaker anticipates that she may become nervous, it's a good idea for her to wear low-heeled shoes to get a firm base for her footing. Leg and knee trembling is usually not noticeable when a speaker wears pants, and many women like to wear a pant suit when giving a talk. If a day-length skirt is worn, it should be full enough to gracefully cover a woman's knees when she sits.

The overall thing to remember is to wear something appropriate—but a little nicer than your everyday clothes. *Talkamatics tip #137: Be sure your grooming—cleanliness of clothes, hair, nails— is faultless.*

## Arranging Your Props

At countdown time, as you arrive for your talk, first look up the chairman. He may wish to discuss a few things.

Then make a final check of your props. Do this even if you advance-scouted a few hours before and found everything in order. Last minute talk-spoilers do sneak in. Here are some do's and don'ts to watch;

1. *Do look at the set-up for your visual aids.* If you use slides, and someone's running the projector for you, talk with him. Have him run off a few slides to make sure they can be seen from all angles of the room. Ideally, you rehearsed with him earlier, but ask him if he has any questions about the script.

2. *Do check on the easel.* If you use a flip pad or other easel material, make sure the easel is present. Sometimes no one's brought it out of the storeroom. Then, make sure it's in the proper place in the room. Put your flip chart on it and test its stability.

I recall a sales executive getting up to address a seminar at Lake Tahoe. He slung his flip chart on an easel, and it collapsed like a couple of matchsticks—all this before 35 people he'd hoped to impress. It took him five minutes to put things back together and the polish was off his talk.

3. *Do note the lectern or table you'll use.* Is the light sufficient to consult your key outline, if need be? If a lectern is used, is *the light too strong?* Carry some Scotch tape and either when you scout beforehand, or when you step up to speak, tape a paper napkin or a piece of paper over the light.

Perhaps you'll want to Scotch-tape your key word outline to the sloping lectern so the outline will stay high enough. What about the height of the lectern?

4. *Do try the microphone*, if you use one. Ask someone in the back of the room if he can hear you. If you have a choice of mikes, ask for a neck mike. Plan to speak in a reasonably loud tone. **Talkamatics tip #138: If a technician is present, ask him to adjust the mike so you'll sound warm and friendly.**

5. *Don't leave any samples or illustrative material around loose before a talk.* One business woman, talking to a group of personnel managers, planned to show personnel kits she'd developed.

She put the kits on the table, and then went to chat with friends before she was to speak.

Fortunately, she checked on the kits a few minutes before her talk. She found most of them missing. People coming into the meeting room thought the material was there to be picked up and helped themselves. She was able to round them up in time for her talk. But it left her rather breathless and flushed when she started her speech.

**Talkamatics tip #139: It's often wise to keep your props, samples, kits and other materials in a suitcase near your chair.** But talk to the program chairman or the dining room captain and ask if the bag will be safe there.

6. *Don't forget to ask the chairman to signal you unobtrusively five minutes before your speaking time is up—unless you rely on a pocket timer.*

## Relaxing Exercises

As you wait to talk, three simple exercises can help you relax:

1. *Swallow a few times.* This moistens your throat.
2. *Yawn several times.* This helps to combat tension.

3. *Breathe deeply.* Push your chest out, tighten your stomach, inhale and exhale. This brings fresh oxygen into your lungs and revitalizes you. I remember the late Bob Weston, a top Boise Cascade executive, when he was leading a two-day meeting, taking every opportunity at the morning and afternoon breaks and lunch time to step out of doors and breathe deeply. Each time after this, he'd mount the platform with new zest.

## Playing the Interested Role

When mingling with people before a meeting, or while you eat dinner and listen to others on the program, it's important to *act as if you're fascinated by the proceedings.*

Sometimes this is difficult to do, as when, for example, club members talk endlessly about a new by-law you couldn't be less concerned with.

However, **Talkamatics tip #140: You must appear interested while waiting to talk.**

It's not only the courteous thing to do, but it's important for three special reasons:

1. *It helps you pre-sell yourself to the audience.* If you look bright and alert, your listeners think: "He'll be a great speaker!" If you look bored, disinterested or scared as you wait your turn, the audience thinks, "He looks bored," or "He looks frightened. I bet he'll be a terrible speaker. Wish I hadn't come. Guess I'll tune out." And they do, without giving you a chance to prove yourself.

2. *Another reason for playing the interested role is you can get info you can use in your own speech.* A personnel assistant, sent out by the home office to explain a new vacation policy to factory employees, first listened as they discussed at length the pros and cons of playing an upcoming factory-league baseball game.

The personnel assistant learned some of the nicknames of the employees and their various playing strengths. He wove these into his talk on the new vacation policy. You can imagine how well his talk went over because of his use of upbeat local references.

3. *The third reason to play the interested role is not only to keep you alert,* so you speak with vitality and force, but to emphasize the essential target-reaching method given earlier—*it keeps your thought off yourself and focused outward.*

Finally, along with playing the interested role in pre-talk time, you'll want to remember this Talkamatics automatic: From time to time, mentally run over your memorized opening to make sure everything's in order.

*Talkamatics tip #141: Every so often, think through, in broad terms, your main points and the illustrations you'll use for them.*

## Platform Pointers

As you sit waiting to speak, on a platform or at a table, remember these pointers:

*Sit tall, in the action posture, described in Chapter 5.* You'll recall that the trunk of your body and your thighs should form a nice straight right angle. Rest your feet flat on the floor. Hold your chin at right angles to your neck. This posture gets you breathing right and feeling bright.

*Look at your audience with friendly interest.* Art Willig, a Wilmington, Delaware convenience store manager told me he likes to think, "My, this group looks interesting." If your thinking is friendly, it'll show in your face.

Don't be like some speakers you've seen who, waiting to speak during a business or dinner meeting, shoot a shy look out at their future  listeners and then let their gaze scurry back to their yellow note pad or plate.

*Talkamatics tip #142: While waiting to give your talk, every so often look at your future audience with friendliness and interest. Smile occasionally.*

## Audience-Pleasing Tricks

Once you've prepared your talk, you're on the threshold of a successful speech. At this point, you'll want to pull out *all* the stops in making a talk because a first-class presentation will help you achieve some first-class career goodies.

So, as you step up to speak, here are what I feel are eight audience-pleasing tricks. Note that number seven is VITAL!

1. Stand up to speak with alacrity, energy, and as if you're *delighted* to do so.

2. Say a simple, sincere "thank you" to your introducer, using his name.

3. Without seeming hurried, but promptly, put down your notes and arrange any visual aids.

**Talkamatics tip #143:** *When you want your audience to quiet down, your standing quietly, expectantly, will do the trick.*

Also this quiet waiting gives your audience time to inventory you. My first speech coach warned me, "Let your listeners get a good look at you. Let them inventory what you look like, what you're wearing, the colors, your shoes, everything Only then will they give their full attention to what you'll say."

4. If you use a throw-away remark—that is, if you wish to reply to something your introducer has said or pay a compliment to your listeners about their accomplishments—do so.

Perhaps you wonder—how do you manage an apt throwaway? It's that old up-the-ladder ingredient: *homework.* When talking to a club, learn some of the club's achievements from the club secretary and refer to them. Example: "I'm happy tonight to talk to the Garden Club that took first place in the recent state contest."

5. Give your memorized opening, speaking in a firm, slightly-louder-than-usual voice. Later you can drop back to the right vocal volume for the group. Use strong eye contact.

6. *And here's the big, big, BIG trick in banishing fear while you actually give your talk.* First, don't worry about any initial nervousness. If you've planned and rehearsed your speech properly, most of your listeners won't be aware of the problem.

In a recent seminar in New York City, 20 uptight executives were videotaped while speaking. When their videotape was replayed, their tension didn't show up on the screen, demonstrating to them that if a speaker's properly prepared, his nervousness is usually not visible to others.

Now, second, this kick-off nervousness will leave and you'll be off and running great IF YOU KEEP YOUR THOUGHT UNDIVIDED AND SOLIDLY ON YOUR SUBJECT ALL THE TIME YOU GIVE YOUR TALK.

7. For even 30 seconds, don't wander down thinking bypaths such as: "Do they like my talk so far? Am I doing well? Gosh, I feel nervous. Can they see me shaking? Why's that fellow frowning at what I say?"

If your thinking strays off your talk subject, yank it back. I like to think of the way a wrestler gets a half nelson on his opponent. When I'm giving a talk I've got a half nelson on my subject and nobody can make me turn loose from focusing *hard* on it.

**Talkamatics tip #144:** *Throw all your energy and concentration on the points you make—and you've got your speech made!*

A college professor, noted as a terrific speaker, got carried away one day as he was lecturing, fell off the platform, didn't stop his talk, continued talking as he climbed back. In other words, he was engrossed in his subject. Think about it. You can be, too. And reap the career pay-offs of subject-centered talking.

8. Guard against using a monotonous tone as if speaking to yourself and unaware of your listeners. If you speak enthusiastically, with your mind 100% on what you say, you'll automatically vary your pace and volume, and become forceful in the more important parts.

And **Talkamatics tip #145:** *A great monotony curber is to talk conversationally "with" rather than "at" your audience.*

Speaker-rattling gremlins creep into the best prepared talks. Sometimes a speaker omits a statistic, a credit line for work, or a main point. What do you do when this happens?

Back up? Apologize to the audience and make the correction? Almost never!

**Talkamatics tip #146:** *About 99% of the time it's better to go ahead as if unaware you omitted something.*

## How to Cope with Boo-Boos

What about a boo-boo? You don't skip a name or a statistic but you give it incorrectly? You cite 40 instead of 50 million families living in their own homes or you mention John Smith first came up with the home buying/selling plan when really it was John Brown. Or what if you find yourself mispronouncing a word?

Should you reverse and correct this? No. A Talkamatics automatic is to continue as if oblivious of the boo-boo. Your listeners may realize your mistake but will understand it's only a verbal slip-up.

Another strong reason for not correcting an omission or boo-boo is that often when you backtrack for a correction, you fluff again.

Occasionally in a company meeting, where others may know some of the figures or names you use, you may say 40 million when you mean 50 million. Then someone in the audience may call out a correction, "Mike, I think you meant to say 50 million." If that happens, just nod, say, "Thank you," repeat "50 million" firmly and go on.

**Talkamatics tip #147:** *It interrupts your audience's train of thought to dwell on a boo-boo.*

## How to Cut for Time Shortages

In Chapter 9, I coached you in timing your talk. But what happens when the unforeseen occurs—a disturbance in the audience, or the previous speaker ran over time? Now you suddenly find your pocket timer or the chairman signalling that you have only five minutes left.

Should you run over time? Let me tell it like it is. Listeners loathe, despise, hate and try to give the "evil eye" to any talker who goes over even *ten seconds* of his allotted time. Now never try to talk faster and cram in all your material. Instead, cut. Review Chapter 9 for tips on hatcheting your talk.

## Ideas for Solving the Unexpected

Besides misstatements and running over time, here are some of the unexpecteds that occur when delivering a speech—and how to solve them:

*Late comers.* Usually it's best to pause and let them get seated. If they can easily reach seats in the back or sides of the room, continue your talk as they take their seats. When the only seats left are down in front, it's often good manners to pause and pleasantly say, "There are a few choice seats here in front," and then stand smiling until they're seated.

*Loud noises.* If you hear an airplane or siren outside, or possibly someone running a lawn mower under an open window, if you can be heard, continue to talk. What if the noise is overpowering? Stop, and wait till it's over or ask if someone will see if the noise can be taken care of.

*Discomforts.* If you notice some form of discomfort— perhaps the room is too hot—ask if someone can look into this.

## Talkamatics-Proved Results in Looking 'em in the Eye.

Bet when you see this heading you groan, "Whaaat? Emphasizing eye contact *again*?" Yes. Just as a golf or tennis pro keeps pounding away at make-the-difference points, Talkamatics does too. You see, while you rehearsed using eye-locking, you could forget to use it when you actually deliver your big talk. But you *mustn't*. You must, without fail, from start to finish, use eye control.

    **Talkamatics tip #148:** *If you give an average talk, but handcuff your gaze to the gaze of your listeners, they'll rate you as a strong, even SUPER SPEAKER.*

## Keep Your Voice Up

As you speak, don't let your voice sink into your chest and become low. This is a common fault in giving a talk.

    **Talkamatics tip #149:** *By looking at your audience, and sending your voice out to various parts of the room, you automatically keep your voice up.*

## The Right Ending Gesture

When you close your talk, include this Talkamatics automatic: Make a warm, friendly, rather large gesture. Often you'll wish to use both hands, perhaps palms upward, gesturing enthusiastically as you give your memorized closing.

People recall your talk by its ending. If you make only a so-so talk, but have a good ending, audiences grade your talk as good!

Remember **Talkamatics tip #150:** *A big definite gesture at the ending will add a lot of strength and vitality to your remarks.*

## How to Respond to Applause

At your speech's close, as you gesture strongly and step forward firmly, you've set up a group to applaud you. And chances are, they will—vigorously. How should you respond? Wait a minute till you can be heard comfortably. Smile, nod, and say simply, "Thank you."

Some speakers like to add, "You've been a great audience," or a variation on this, but it's become more of a cliche than a listener-pleaser. So it makes a better overall pattern just to say "Thank you," and not give the impression you'll launch into another talk.

However, once you go across the finish line of a talk, your responsibility is not over. You often need to field a question-and-answer session. And today, again because of increased communication and the impact of television, you must handle your question-and-answer session like a pro. The next chapter will show you how.

## Chapter Check-Back

• *Loving Thy Listeners* consists of feeling gratitude and appreciation for your audience.

• *Advance scouting* of the premises, a day or so before the talk, is advisable. See if what you'll need—table or lectern, easel, blackboard, perhaps a mike, as well as what the group will need: note pads, ballpoints, carafe of drinking water—will be available.

• *Wearing the right clothes* when you give a talk often means wearing a "good" version of your everyday apparel. Be sure your grooming is impeccable.

• *Arranging your props* on arrival includes last-minute checking on the "workability" of the easel, slide projector, mike, etc. Don't leave samples or illustrative material lying around loose for others to grab, thinking they are hand-outs.

• *Relaxing exercises*—swallowing, yawning, and breathing deeply—can help overcome tension.

• *Playing the interested role* is vital because (a) it helps you pre-sell yourself to the audience, (b) you often gain information with which to enliven your speech and (c) it's a target-reaching method to keep your thoughts off yourself and focused outward.

• *Mentally running over your memorized opening* and the broad outlines of the main points and illustrations is recommended.

• *Audience-pleasing tips:* Look at your listeners and wait until you have everyone's attention before starting to talk; give your memorized opening in an extra-loud voice; talk conversationally; keep your thought glued to your subject as you speak.

• *Correcting an omission or boo-boo.* If one occurs, usually continue as though unaware you slipped up. Trying to rectify a mistake often causes a worse fluff.

• *Giving a strong ending gesture*—using your hands in a warm, friendly way—is vital.

• *Stepping forward as you make your closing statement* marks a professional speaker.

• *Responding to applause* with a smile and a simple "Thank you" is the right way to close your speech.

**Eleven**

# Adroitly Field Questions and Answers with Talkamatics

An authority on speaking points out that talks are getting shorter and question-and-answer periods longer. Furthermore, audiences relish the new set-up!

Yet, like other facets of successful talking, a Q&A session must be fielded expertly or it can result in an amateurish, career-crippling performance.

In the last chapter, you saw that for a strong finish you should step or lean forward. Now here are two automatics to follow when inviting spoken questions:

1. Again, take a step forward, or if at a lectern or table, lean forward. This body language helps induce questions.

2. When you ask for questions with a comment like, "We've a few minutes for questions. Who has a question?" *raise your own hand*, as if you were querying.

Hold your hand high, so all in the audience can see it. Then, keeping your hand high in the air, look around for the first questioner. If talking to a small group of eight or less people, follow these procedures—but you needn't raise your hand as high.

*Talkamatics tip #151: This body language—stepping or leaning forward and raising your hand—will do much to kick off your Q&A session successfully.*

## A Ladder-Climbing Case History

I recall how learning to kick off a Q&A helped Gary Parcher continue up the corporate ladder. Gary, a newly promoted divisional manager in a paper company in New York City, found he must now give talks to clubs, civic and campus groups.

Gary's talks? Passable. But his Q&A periods? Disasters! Questions dried up. Listeners complained his Q&As were "uninteresting."

Disturbed by these complaints, the company president urged Gary to take speaking lessons. He did so. His speech coach diagnosed much of Gary's Q&A trouble as, after asking for the first question, he stepped backward. After the second question, the coach pointed out, Gary again stepped backward. And by the next question, if anyone bothered to ask it, Gary was hugging the room wall or auditorium curtain.

"You reject your audience," said the coach. "By stepping backward you signal your wish to escape. No wonder your listeners don't ask questions, and no wonder you aren't winning friends and supporters for your company's programs."

After a month of diligent work, Gary could give an enthusiastic speech and warmly step forward and invite questions. His stepping forward was so vigorous and showed such interest in his listeners that hands shot up...and it became apparent Gary's acceptance as a speaker had increased tremendously.

**Talkamatics tip #152:** *Knowing how to invite questions is part of persuasive speaking.*

## Courteous Manners Your Secret Weapon

Courteous manners can be a secret weapon in a Q&A period. But how do you display friendly manners? Several ways. Among them:

- Smiling as you recognize the questioners.
- Looking interested as you listen to the question.

• Answering in an attentive way—never ridiculing or making fun of the question or questioner.

• Remaining unflappable even if someone appears to bait you.

*Talkamatics tip #153: Your best defense in fielding questions is a friendly, polite approach to your listeners under all circumstances.*

However, many talkers say they possess an affable manner but listeners fail to ask them questions. What's the remedy? The Talkamatics target-reaching method is simple.

## Preparing Talkamatics Prime-the-Pump Questions

Before making a talk, you should prepare two to four questions you can toss out yourself. While you break the ice, your listeners have time to think and prepare questions.

Here's how the Talkamatics prime-the-pump technique works.

When you remark you'll be glad to answer questions and don't notice a hand shooting up, say:

"While you get ready, I'd like to ask a question—and answer it, myself."

Or: "And while you think of your questions, here's something that may puzzle you."

Then ask a question your speech might have raised but not answered.

If the audience still seems to be thinking, ask another provocative question to stir them up. By provocative, what do I mean? Something that will stimulate people to ask questions. For example, in Mike Williams' home-buying speech, he might prime the pump for the Q&A session with:

"While I've told you the good things about the home-buying plan, *I'd* like to ask a question—and answer it myself. Are there any drawbacks to this plan? Has anyone moved out of a home in Centerville, instead of buying it? Actually, someone did...."

Or another provocative question:

"Although I told you about saving money by this plan, some of you may wonder, 'Did anybody lose money? And how much?' Well, to be frank...."

### "Complete Break" Turning Away

To win your stripes in handling Q&As, you need to know Talkamatics complete-break rules. These include:

1. *To start off, always recognize the questioner by turning to face him.*

2. *Next—and this is IMPORTANT—always turn from the questioner in a complete break after you hear the question.*

3. *Then, facing another (usually the major) portion of your listeners, repeat the question loudly enough so everyone can hear it.*

Generally, follow this technique even when talking to a small group. Why? For several reasons. First, repeating the question allows you thinking time. In the few seconds you turn to another portion of your listeners and repeat the question, your subconscious starts to hammer out an answer. Your subconscious will come up with a neater answer than if you heard the question and, *bango!*, answered it.

Second, by repeating (and if necessary, rephrasing the question for clarity), you make sure that everyone gets to hear it. And third, when you repeat the question in a strong voice, you flatter the questioner. You treat his question with dignity and importance. You get him on your side!

### Avoiding an Audience-Boring Debate

What's *another* reason Talkamatics urges the complete break? If you continue to face the questioner, he may quickly ask you another question, you answer and he pops another question. Before you know it, you're into a question/answer ping-pong match—or even worse, a debate. Nothing bores listeners more than you and one of your listeners playing ye olde high school debaters. Often your listeners can't hear your dialog, and would-be questioners chafe at being ignored.

> ***Talkamatics tip #154:*** *Don't allow an audience-boring debate to begin. When you speak, keep the power in your own hands.*

And here's a caution: Try not to turn back to the questioner and ask, "Does that answer your question?" Assume your reply does. If the questioner desires more facts, he'll talk to you after the meeting.

Sometimes in a company meeting, however, you must answer several questions from the same person to clarify a point.

> ***Talkamatics tip #155:*** *Generally, the name of the question game is variety—one question per person from various people, in various parts of the room.*

## Skipping Those No-No Phrases

When answering queries, avoid a few audience-irritating phrases. Among them:

a) *"I don't follow you."* Sounds testy. You might rephrase it to: "I'm afraid I don't understand your point."

b) *"That's irrelevant."* Instead say something like: "I'm afraid my research hasn't taken me into that area. Sorry."

c) *"I covered that. Didn't you hear me?"* Instead you might comment: "I believe I touched on that. But in a nutshell..." and then repeat the point very briefly.

d) *"Well, that'd take too long to answer."* You might reply: "That would take too long for the question time allotted us but I'd be happy to discuss it with you on a one-to-one basis after this meeting."

e) *"I'm not at liberty to say."* You could rephrase to: "For several reasons, I can't answer that at this time. But I can tell you one thing..." and answer part of the question. If you can't answer all the question, a little information often is appreciated.

While this chapter so far has shown you remarks to avoid, how exactly should you answer questions from the audience?

## The 1-2-3 Magic Package Answer

In a question session, audiences want direct answers. **Talkamatics tip #156: *Never fabricate a false answer.*** When you don't know an answer, admit it. If feasible, promise you'll find out and get in touch with the questioner later.

A target-reacher way to answer is with the 1-2-3 Magic Package module you first learned in Chapter 2. Here's how to apply it in a Q&A session.

To get back to our friend Mike Williams. Someone asks him:

"I understand, Mike, the new home-buying plan laid an egg in Houston. And I've heard that about 15 families got stung. Please comment."

Mike gives the 1-2-3 Magic Package answer. His first sentence is a statement of fact.

1. "No, I'm sorry, Bill, you're mistaken; there's been just *one* case reported when a home buyer wasn't satisfied."

The second part of the 1-2-3 Magic Package answer gives a specific, a statistic, an anecdote or something out of his own experience that enlarges on his first sentence. Thus:

2. "An executive and his family in Houston had moved into a house with a $250 monthly rental. But because the wife likes a fireplace and the house had none, the family decided not to apply the monthly rental towards buying the house, but to move out."

By giving some specific details in this middle section, Mike convinces his listeners he knows what he's talking about. They tend to believe him. Yet, notice, he doesn't give too much detail that would tire his audience. Mike then goes on to the wind-up in his 1-2-3 Magic Package answer which often gives a recommendation.

3. "In fact, Bill, based on some cases I observed closely, I'd recommend this home-buying plan to any executive."

You may say, "Sure, it's fine to use the 1-2-3 Magic Package answer, and give specific detail in the middle portion of the answer. But how do I pull this specific detail out of the blue?"

The answer is that you don't pull it out of the blue. *You anticipate questions.* Also, when you rehearse your speech you tell your listeners—such as your spouse or business friends—what kind of audience you'll speak before, and to frame the type of questions that audience will ask. Then stockpile specific information to answer these questions.

And **Talkamatics tip #157** is *keep this evidence—such as a statistic or quote—with the place marked beside you and read this evidence to your listeners, citing your authority.*

By the way, the more educated your audience the more specific evidence you'll want to use in answering questions.

## Graceful Getaways from Embarrassing Questions

When you're up front answering questions, you're fair game. You never know who'll take a potshot at you and ask a question that could embarrass you or your company. How do you handle explosive-type questions?

- Assume your questioner's good faith;
- Answer honestly and candidly wherever possible;
- Impersonalize some answers; and
- Keep your cool with hecklers.

**1. Assume your questioner's good faith.** Questioners may query for various reasons—ranging from wanting information to desiring to show up, or even make a personal attack on, you or your company. However, you must assume your questioner is asking in good faith. And actually, most questions you get will be this kind.

**2. Answer honestly and candidly whenever possible.** I recall being in a writing class taught by my friend Frank Dana of San Diego, California. Frank is a leading business magazine writer. A beginning writer suddenly asked Frank how much money he made a year.

Instead of giving an untrue figure, or hedging, Frank candidly replied:

"Each year, for the past five years, I paid tax on declared income in excess of $20,000. Aside from a small amount of interest from a savings account, my income came from writing."

Frank's honesty was so apparent everyone in the class felt he would tell the truth on future writing questions asked him.

**3. When remarks get personal, impersonalize your answers.** Sometimes a speaker will receive an embarrassing question to answer. Often it's ticklish because it's tied to a personality. For example, someone might say to Mike Williams, the manager of the real-estate development mentioned earlier: "I hear Tom Allison (a rival developer) tried a plan similar to yours about five years ago and lost his shirt. Will you please comment?"

Impersonalize your reply. You might say something like: "Sorry, I don't know enough about that situation to comment. I might say, however, three leading developers in other parts of the country tried the plan successfully. Would you like to know their names? Then please see me afterward. In fact, I've a chart showing their rate of business increase which might interest you."

**4. Handling a hostile audience.** Today business people face more hostile audiences than formerly. To illustrate: An executive of a telephone or oil company often must field questions about rate increases or other queries from riled listeners.

So *Talkamatics tip #158: As advised earlier, it's important to anticipate before a Q&A period the audience's viewpoint and questions.*

In addition, remember these two points:

a) You must give a hostile audience hope that something can be done. One show-you: If Mike Williams, the development manager mentioned before, found hostility surfacing in a question-and-answer period, with someone suddenly asking why his development was widening a road and cutting down beautiful trees, he wouldn't merely answer, "Because the auto traffic necessitated this." He would add something hopeful.

He might explain, "Actually, we'll save five trees and we're planting new trees which eventually will line both sides of the road."

b) A leader doesn't last long with a negative approach. When you step up to give a talk, you embark on a leadership step. ***Talkamatics tip #159: Accent positive values in your Q&A period.***

**5. Dealing with hecklers.** Sometimes in a Q&A session a noisy heckler, or even a group of hecklers, will make loud, uncomplimentary remarks.

Speak to the troublemaker, or the group, in a calm voice. Request quiet so you can both hear and answer their questions.

***Talkamatics tip #160: A quiet, unexcited manner can often help subdue the noisy heckler. You don't want to end up in a shouting match.***

Keep bringing any exchange with hecklers back to *facts*, using specifics—such as statistics, examples and case histories—to prove your point

***Talkamatics tip #161: When answering hecklers, remain unemotional and courteous, and answer their questions factually.***

Draw the session to a close as soon as possible.

However, a group of hecklers may go further than making derogatory remarks. They may bring out banners and placards, stand up, and even march around the room. If this happens, ask them to resume their seats so the audience can hear what's going on.

**Talkamatics tip #162:** *If the hecklers continue, it's wise to cut off your remarks and leave the platform.* Today there's no stigma in exiting like this. Nevertheless, the majority of audiences will not pose the problem of hecklers bent on creating chaos.

## Helpful Hints for Answering Company Meeting Questions

Every so often you may be called upon to give a talk to your fellow employees. For instance, you may tell them of a new procedure your department is adopting and ask for their cooperation; or you may explain your work and how it fits into the overall company program.

In company meetings, when answering questions keep alert to these target-reaching techniques:

*Seldom use the first-person pronoun, "I".* Instead, use the word "we" and "our team" or "our group." **Talkamatics tip #163:** *When you single yourself out enough to be asked to talk about your work in a company meeting, and use "I" heavily, co-workers may feel you're building yourself up.* But if you call it a plan or procedure worked out by "our group," or "our team," your listeners, some of whom may have helped develop the plan or procedure, will feel warmly toward you.

*Try not to let personalities—especially in a derogatory sense—creep into your answers.* Watch that you don't say: "If Ed Matthews' shipping room doesn't fall behind, we can now get the order out on time."

Maybe the shipping room does fall behind quite a bit and Ed Matthews is accountable. But you need not pass judgment on departments and people in this briefing session. Be impersonal and say something like: "With the shipping room's cooperation, we now can get the orders out as scheduled."

*Don't give out information you're not authorized to.* Perhaps you've described a new plan to deliver appliances by truck from the factory to distributors. Suddenly someone veers off the truck delivery subject and asks the question, "Harvey, I hear we'll start giving rebates to customers. How will this rebating work?"

Watch out! ***Talkamatics tip #164: In a Q&A session, don't reveal unauthorized information.*** You may know your company will rebate shortly, but you're not authorized to give out this information. Yet you don't want to fib and say, "I haven't heard anything about that," when you have.

What should you do? You might look at the questioner and say something like, "Well, of course that announcement would come from Mr. Bascomb. I understand he'll drop in a little later but I don't know what it's in reference to."

*Accentuate the positive benefits.* Always stress positive benefits rather than dwell on negative aspects in answering company meeting questions.

If someone complains that your new truck delivery plan will mean staggered lunch hours, thus disrupting the shipping room crew's lunch-hour baseball game, acknowledge the criticism. But point out that under the new plan each shipping room worker will also get more *flex* time every week, so he can take care of personal business more handily.

## Closing a Q&A Session

You'll note that in most Q&A periods, questions usually get off to a rather slow start, then they become more spontaneous, frequently reach a peak of interest, and finally begin to taper off.

So ***Talkamatics tip #165*** is, *generally speaking, when you see the peak of interest has passed, cut off the Q&A session.*

Often this question time is about ten minutes. However, if you're talking to an interested group, you can let the questions run to 15 or 20 minutes. In a company meeting, in order to answer every possible question, you may need to continue as long as your listeners want to query you.

But above all, if questions become sparse, don't stand searching the room for a possible additional remark. And don't ask someone who looks as if he might have a question if he'd like to ask one. This only irritates a busy audience who'd rather leave and use the time for something else.

To close a Q&A session, simply say, "I'm sorry but this is all the time we have for questions. However, if anybody wishes to talk with me, I'll be here for a few minutes. Thank you."

Adroitly fielding questions after a speech helps stamp you as a professional in speaking. Yet to uphold your reputation as a deft talker you need to learn certain tips for finding subjects and illustrations. The next chapter will help provide this expertise.

## Chapter Check-Back

• *Stepping or leaning forward* and raising your own hand high, as if asking a question yourself, are two Talkamatics automatics that encourage questions from your listeners.

• *Displaying warm, courteous manners,* never ridiculing a question or questioner, and remaining unflappable when baited, pleases audiences at a Q&A session.

• *Preparing from two to four prime-the-pump questions* that you or a friend in the audience can ask, will start things rolling.

• *Turning from the questioner* with a complete break and then repeating the question to your audience is requisite before answering the question. Sometimes you must rephrase the question for clarity. . -

• *Avoiding an audience-boring debate?* Two tips for doing so: Don't ask, "Does that answer your question?" Also refrain from turning back to the same questioner and letting him pose another question.

• *Ping-ponging remarks* from the same questioner to the speaker often can't be heard by everyone. They cause listeners to y-a-w-n.

• *An answering rule of thumb,* taught by Talkamatics, is one question per person, and a variety of questions from all segments of the group. However, sometimes in a company meeting you must answer more than one question from the same person to clear up certain points.

• *Skipping no-no phrases* like "I don't follow you" or "That's irrelevant" will win friends among listeners and questioners.

• *Using the 1-2-3 Magic Package answer* — the first sentence a statement of fact, the second part a specific, the wind-up a recommendation—will please listeners.

• *Achieving a graceful getaway from embarrassing questions* includes answering honestly, impersonalizing some answers, emphasizing any hopeful aspects with hostile questioners, and keeping your cool with hecklers.

• *Adroitly fielding company meeting questions* means weeding out the pronoun "I," and derogatory references to company personalities, giving out only information you're authorized to, and accentuating the positive benefits of a plan or procedure.

## Twelve

# The Talkamatics Easy Path
# to Finding Subjects
# and Illustrations

To become a vital talker, you must come up with absorbing subjects and illustrative material. This chapter contains tips on how to lay your hands on blue chip material for presentations.

## Fishing in Your Overflowing Day

As you read a memo, browse through a trade or general magazine, talk with a business associate or friend, think of yourself as also doing a little fishing on the side.

When you spot a possible idea for a future presentation, reel in that idea. Ditto when you come across a Talkamatics dazzler—anecdote, story, example, analogy, statistic, fact—that might illustrate a future talk. Pull in the dazzler.

The trick, though, is to catch these treasures *fast*—before they swim away.

## The Little Notebook System

I've found one of the best ways to reel in this material is with a 3″ x 5″ ringed notebook with removable pages. Regularly, at the end or beginning of each day, jot down that amusing story or copy a striking statistic from a memo. The

emphasis is on *regularly*. Don't delay or do this only occasionally or good material will escape—and you'll be the
talker who apologizes, "I had a great statistic to prove my
point but couldn't lay my hands on it."

## Some Basic Subjects That Delight Audiences

Here are seven categories of subjects I found go over big
with audiences. Often by pondering these subjects you'll hit
on an idea for a talk. Then, by molding your remarks to your
listeners' interests, you can deliver a stand-out presentation.

### 1. Telling what something is.

This type of speech *describes* something—in an intriguing manner. For example:

- Your job responsibility
- Your department's function
- Your committee's activities
- Your company's most important activities
- Your company's fringe benefits
- Your hobby of flower photography (or other hobby)
- Your vacation trip to Nova Scotia (or other area)

### 2. Describing how to do it.

In this category, you would emphasize *how* to do it—
giving a step-by-step method.

- A job function
- An improved procedure on the job
- Upgrading a job skill
- Drafting a good business report
- Profitably attending a workshop or night school class
- Jogging (or other exercise) for fitness
- Raising funds for a worthy cause
- Taking mini vacations

### 3. Tying in with a special occasion.

Perhaps you'll say a few words at a birthday lunch in honor of your boss, at a bowling league end-of-season dinner, or a meeting of your state's dentists. With a little skull work, you can interestingly tie in your talk with the occasion. For example:

*Your boss' birthday:*

- Your recollections of your boss when you first came to work
- Memories of others about the guest of honor
- Predictions of how the guest of honor will continue to achieve fame

*At a bowling league dinner:*

- The real reasons why your team placed as it did
- Five foolproof ways you learned this season to throw a bowling ball
- Tips that will liberate women bowlers

*Before a professional group:*

- Who is a good dentist? (employee? boss? accountant? teacher?)
- What I look for in a supplier (dentist, salesman, accountant, teacher)
- How to please a client (customer, student, patient)

### 4. Relating the story of (in narrative form)

- Designing one of your company's products
- Making rubber (or other material) products
- A particular business recession
- Early days in business

- The growth of minority lawyers (doctors, journalists, business people, etc.)
- How the Chamber of Commerce was founded

## 5. Pointing out the reasons for (analysis)

- A new organizational plan
- A product's success in the market place
- A winning merchandising method
- Tax breaks to business
- Your area's hurricanes
- Your local energy crisis
- Your town's pollution
- An industry leader's genius

## 6. Relating history/biography/autobiography

- The first business firm in the U.S.
- The first printing (accounting, newspaper,manufacturing, etc.) business in the U.S.
- The first profit-sharing plan in American industry
- The early commercial airlines
- A colorful leader in business (in whatever field you wish to speak about)
- Quotes from a great industrialist's autobiography
- A businessman turned prominent politician

## 7. Speaking about "the arts"

- Business firms' interest in the arts
- Your firm's gifts to encourage the arts
- Your fellow employees' participation in the arts
- "Arts" hobbies of members of your trade association
- How the kids of your fellow employees are rising in the arts
- Business people with musical hobbies
- Profitable collecting for business people

## Vividizing Your Talk

Once you select your subject, you can choose Talkamatics dazzlers from your pocket notebook for illustrations. However, you may need specific dazzlers your notebook doesn't provide. Here's how to turn up specific talk illustrations...

## Five Gold Mines of Fresh Stories

Most good speakers rate apt, fresh anecdotes as a superb way to illustrate a talk. Here are five gold mines for finding sparkling new stories:

1. *Your own background.*

2. *The experience of your* business associates, friends, family, relatives.

3. *Business biographies.* Form a habit of reading interviews with business people in:

> *The New York Times, The Christian Science Monitor* and other leading newspapers.
> *Forbes, Business Week, Fortune, Time, Nation's Business,* etc.

Clip intriguing anecdotes. Sometimes you may want to fictionize the anecdote by changing the name of the person, the locale, industry, etc., to make it fit *your* talk.

4. *Trade magazines.* Save the anecdotal material in your trade magazines. Don't use this material if you talk to an industry group which reads these magazines. However, if you speak to a civic group and can adapt these stories to your audience's interest, your stories will sound unique and lively.

5. *Books.* When you read a business book, history or biography, and come to an arresting case history or anecdote, don't just savor it—mark and later copy it. If necessary, change details—such as names, occupations, products—and

come up with a Talkamatics dazzler suitable for your purpose.

## Tailoring Your Stories to Your Listeners

In illustrating a talk, here are a few pointers on customizing your stories for your audience.

1. *Make story people like listeners* whenever possible. A business person likes to hear a story about another business person. Even more precisely a mechanical engineer will drink in an account about another M.E., a councilman about another councilman, an editor about another editor. So when feasible, change your anecdotal characters to resemble your listeners. Examples: Change a story set in San Mateo, California, to Sioux City, Iowa, or from the garment business to the fast food business.

2. *Use local references.* If you make a talk to employees at one of your company's factories, scan several issues of the factory house organ. Note what's going on. Work these items into your talk. Talking to a club or civic group? Get several back copies of their newsletter and do the same thing.

3. *Weave in listeners' names.* Telling an anecdote with a couple of characters? Why not use the names of two of the people in the audience. (Check with them first to see if it's okay to do so.) The anecdote will sound about 1000 times as interesting to that group!

## A Quick Guide to Securing Statistics

Statistics add nuts and raisins of interest to your talk. See Figure 2.

## Making Statistics Fascinating

Once you collect some statistics, edit them.

1. *Select the most dramatic.*

2. *Put them in recognizable terms.* Don't just say, for example, the U.S. boasts over 200,000 millionaires. But make the statement more meaningful with a remark like, "There

| People | Print |
|---|---|
| Your company department of:<br>   Accounting<br>   Public Relations<br>   Personnel<br>   Safety<br>   Sales | Trade/business/ professional magazines.<br>*The U.S. Census.*<br>Reference books at your business or local library. |
| People in your trade/business/ professional association.<br>People in city, state, U.S. government and private agencies.<br>Educators, librarians. | Material prepared by city, state, U.S. government and private agencies.<br>*Statistical Abstract of the United States* gives statistics on social, political and economic organizations, from agriculture to trucking. |

**Figure 2: WHERE TO GET STATISTICAL INFORMATION**

are over 200,000 millionaires in the U.S., enough to make up the population of _____(name a nearby city of 200,000)."

3. *Round off statistics.* Usually it's more effective to round off statistics to the nearest hundred, thousand, hundred thousand or million.

4. *Always use statistics sparingly.* Too many figures weary your listeners.

## Finding Just the Facts, Ma'am

Quite often you need facts to sparkle your talk. You might want some biographical information, the dates of a business enterprise, a juicy quotation. Where do you find them?

## Your Own Resources

In speaking, some of your best facts come from your own resources. These include:

1. *Your own background.* Example: If you speak about the energy crisis, often facts you give about its effects on your own family, business or town, will produce far more impact than those you read up on for your talk.

A telephone executive told me that one day he wanted facts to show a group of listeners that they were still getting a "bargain" in telephone rates. He listed phone calls his family made that day for handling family business, and totaled up the *time* these calls took, plus the *cost*.

He then listed the time, plus what it would have cost for gasoline, postage, writing materials, etc., if this same family business had been handled in person or by mail. The telephone transactions were more economical...and he proved his point resoundingly.

Listeners value remarks from your own background, so shuffle through your experiences and pull out any pertinent information.

Also, when fact-seeking, check:

2. *Your own files of correspondence, memos, newsletters, booklets, magazines.*

One time, when I was with Boise Cascade recreational communities, I beefed to an exec that I'd have to get on the Wats line and round up some facts—when the communities were started, their size, amenities, etc.—for an upcoming talk. He chuckled, then said, "I can save you some work. Remember, almost everything of importance in any company has been written down at some time or another." He added, "Talk to some key secretaries. They'll hunt up those facts. You don't need to re-gather them." He was right. I chopped off a couple of days' work.

## Pointers on Library Looking

Before talking to your local library's reference librarian (who'll unearth files, pamphlets, suggest articles and books with meaty facts), you may wish to research on your own. See Sources for Facts (Figure 3).

**Sources for Facts**

| Reference Books | Periodical Indexes | Miscellaneous |
|---|---|---|
| Encyclopedias will give you a quick overview of a subject. Two useful encyclopedias:<br>• *The Encyclopedia Britannica*<br>• *The Encyclopedia Americana*<br><br>*Standard & Poor's Directories* will give you firms' type of business, name and address, names of top executives, etc.<br><br>*Who's Who* series. There are a number of useful *Who's Who* books including *Who's Who* in business and industry, the arts, clergy, in New York, etc.<br><br>*Famous First Facts* by Joseph Nathan Kane describes "firsts—from the first airmail service to the first vending machine. | *The Wall Street Journal Index* provides corporate profit reports.<br><br>*Business Periodical Index.* A subject index of business articles—on everything from annual exhibits to the zinc industry.<br><br>*Readers' Guide to Periodical Literature.* Lists by subject matter general-interest articles published by major magazines.<br><br>*The New York Times Index* will help you locate data and information on thousands of subjects, places and people. Great for talk makers to consult! | *Vital Speeches of the Day.* This semimonthly publication available at your library, or by subscription from the City News Publishing Co., Box 606, Southold, N.Y., 11971, contains outstanding speeches. You can study how the top speakers use material and also often find facts you can use in your own speaking.<br><br>*Books in Print* lists thousands of books—general, scientific, industrial—by title, author and subject matter.<br><br>*Phone books* of various cities are often found in your library's reference department. These give you names of companies and businesses you can contact for further information. |

**Figure 3**

## Here's How to Contact Associations, Agencies, Bureaus

1. Trade/business/professional associations bloom with useful information. You can pluck it by contacting an association's director or reference departments. For a run-down on associations, including the director's name and the group's address, consult the *Encyclopedia of Associations*. This thick directory lists non-profit organizations of the U.S. according to interests, as well as foreign groups of concern to Americans, and some local and regional groups, including citizens action groups, projects and programs.

2. *U.S. Government Manual.* You can obtain this at your library or for $5.75 from the Supt. of Documents, Government Printing Offices, Washington, D.C. 20402. This manual lists government agencies and bureaus—such as the Department of Health, Education and Welfare and the Department of Agriculture. You also can get on the mailing list for the "Monthly Catalog of U.S. Government Publications" put out by the Supt. of Documents. This gives the titles of new first-rate pamphlets—on a variety of subjects—which you can order.

Also in the above manual, you'll find the addresses and phone numbers of Small Business Administration offices throughout the country. If you're making a business talk, a local office can often furnish some fascinating facts.

## Useful Sources

Newspapers and magazines can supply you with intriguing facts and figures.

1. *Local newspaper offices* keep files on many subjects in the news. Just visit the newspaper library or "morgue," and ask to see their file of clippings on the subject you need. Often you can photocopy a clipping. Or perhaps the newspaper will allow you to bring in a tape recorder or portable typewriter and make notes.

2. *Magazine booklets.* Many magazines publish information about good booklets available from manufacturers and from industrial and professional groups. Sometimes a letter and a small sum to cover mailing costs will bring you a treasure trove of specifics for a talk.

3. *Books.* Many times you can get Talkamatics dazzlers as well as ideas for planning, illustrating and delivering presentations from books. Here are a few favorites of mine:

• *New Book of Unusual Quotations* (rev. ed.), Rudolf F. Flesch. Harper & Row, New York, 1966.

• *Just for Laughs*, Jack Faulhaber (edited by Jack Irwin). Doubleday & Co., Inc., 1960. This talk sparker contains 2500 jokes, situations and punch lines.

• *Business Ideas: How to Create and Present Them*, Stephen S. Price. Harper & Row, 1967.

• *How to Put Yourself Across with Key Words and Phrases*, Martha W. Cresci. Parker Publishing Co., West Nyack, N.Y., 1973. Here's a book with "magic phrases" to help you move up in the business world.

• *Effective Presentations*, Edward Hodnett. Parker Publishing Co., West Nyack, N.Y.,1967. A fine systematic approach to the process of making presentations. Shows you how to present facts, figures and ideas with professional flair.

• *How to Conduct a Meeting*, The Dun & Bradstreet Business Library, New York, 1969. Good checklists, charts, forms and pointers.

• *How to Talk Your Way to the Top*, Edward J. Hegarty. Parker Publishing Co., West Nyack, N.Y., 1973. Easy, fun to read. Loaded with talking tips that work.

• *How to Stand Up and Speak Well in Business*, Frank Snell. Citadel Press, New York, 1962. A slim book but hefty helps for putting across your ideas.

• *The Negotiator: A Manual for Winners*, Royce A. Coffin. Amacom, New York, 1973. A captivating cartoon book with captions that make the negotiation messages go down easy as ice cream.

• *Executive's Guide to Effective Speaking and Writing*, Frederick C. Dyer. Prentice-Hall, Inc., Englewood Cliffs, N.J., 1962. Good pointers and case histories in sharpening your communication skills.

• *Writing with Style: Conversations on the Art of Writing*, John R. Trimble. Prentice-Hall, Inc., 1975. A mere 138 fast-moving and fun pages that take the mystery out of writing. It'll aid you in drafting fascinating presentations and talks.

## Free Slides and Films

Often, when making a presentation, you'll need slides or film to illustrate your points. Why not take advantage of some free sources?

**Convention and tourist bureaus.** In many cities such bureaus either have material available or can give you tips for obtaining it. Ask for illustrative matter rather than film. If you request film, the bureaus may say they don't have any. But if you ask for illustrative matter to illustrate your presentation, a bureau may come up with film strips or slides.

**Airlines.** Contact the local or national sales manager and ask him if he has visual aids you can borrow on a subject, such as an area's industries or outstanding attractions.

By thinking innovatively, you often can pinpoint an area the airline services that might provide the kind of visual material you need. Some how-to-do-its: Maybe you plan to talk about over-populated cities. Ask an airline if they can supply you with illustrative material on dense metropolitan skylines. Giving a garden talk? An airline that services Portland, Oregon (the City of Roses), might lend you shots of spectacular roses.

**Telephone company.** Call the public relations office of your local company, tell them about the type of illustrative material you're looking for, and ask if they can supply it.

Example: For a talk on women in outdoor jobs, they may be able to provide you with footage (and perhaps facts, too!) on female hard hat employees. Or, if you plan to talk about tulips to a garden club, ask your local telephone company if they'll contact the telephone company in Holland, Michigan, on your behalf. You may be surprised how quickly they'll help you get material.

**Your local library.** More and more libraries have a film department with a collection that can be borrowed. Also the department can give you tips on other sources for visual material. Library films are popular so make arrangements in advance.

**Travel films.** Perhaps you intend to speak about a branch of your company that's opened in the Pennsylvania Dutch Country and would like to show illustrations of the colorful area. Check the local chamber of commerce and the state tourist office for visuals.

**Trade/business/professional associations.** Often a phone call or letter to an association can bring you good illustrative material.

**Professional film distributors.** You'll see these listed in the Yellow Pages of medium and large cities under a heading like "Film Distributors." Their clients include airlines, tourist bureaus, various cities, tourist attractions, etc. They may provide you with visuals free of charge; all you'll have to pay is return postage. Or sometimes, for a small fee, they will offer you a film print.

## Free Artwork

Require artwork, lettering, drawings, charts—and there's no money in the budget? You can often obtain these free from the following sources:

1. *Your company's art department.*
2. *Your company's advertising or public relations manager.* I've touched on this before but a key thing is to

point out to the manager that you don't possess a visual aid budget. Sometimes he has extra money in his budget which he can use to help you out, and his ad or PR agency will quote him a very reasonable price on this type of job.

## Right Paid Sources for Charts, Slides, Prestype

If you decide to buy professional charts, slides or cards with printed messages to illustrate your talk, ask your company advertising or PR manager, or someone you know in the advertising business, to recommend firms that do good work at reasonable prices.

Often I find it pays to shop around among the names one gets. If you find a firm which is not too busy at that time, you'll often receive a lower price estimate.

Another way to hold the estimate down is to explain to a supplier the content of the audience you'll talk to. If it's a small-group, one-time-use only of the illustrative material, and you want something simple but tasteful, often you can secure a better price quote than if a firm is under the impression that you have a large budget and want all the stops pulled out in preparing your visual materials.

## Talkamatics Way to File for Fast Retrieval of Research

A problem you may face is how to file research so you can lay your hands quickly on anecdotes, statistics, quotations and illustrations (such as pictures you might cut out from a catalog, to illustrate a future presentation).

Today the best thinking on filing is *fewer* and *fatter* files. Merely set up a few general category headings and pop in *all* your materials.

About every six weeks or so I go through my files. Time's perspective shows me any duplicate material or items that are not really that great, and also reveals some gems to keep.

Once a year I weed out anything whiskery or less pertinent. The one file I let run is my anecdote file. I hang onto this material and use it year after year.

## You're Moving Towards Your Talkamatics Treasures—Praise, Pay Raises and Promotion

At the end of the first chapter, I pointed out you were at Day One, ready to learn and apply the Talkamatics system in every aspect of your communication with others.

Now you know bull's-eye methods for hitting your talking targets. Already you've put some speaking principles into practice. You plan to utilize other Talkamatics guidelines. Let me urge you to do this as quickly as possible.

Keep structuring your remarks on the 1-2-3 Magic Package module. Continue to apply these rules in your presentations and talks.

In the Bible, the book of Deuteronomy states the goals of those striving upward in these simple terms:

"The Lord shall make thee the head, and not the tail, and thou shalt not be beneath...."

You'll find embodying the new Talkamatics methods is the easy way to verbal power and persuasion, and can help take you up the ladder fast, faster, fastest.